FROM WALES

Edited by Lucy Jenkins

First published in Great Britain in 2000 by
YOUNG WRITERS
Remus House,
Coltsfoot Drive,
Woodston,
Peterborough, PE2 9JX
Telephone (01733) 890066

All Rights Reserved

Copyright Contributors 2000

HB ISBN 0 75431 858 3
SB ISBN 0 75431 859 1

FOREWORD

This year, the Young Writers' Future Voices competition proudly presents a showcase of the best poetic talent from over 42,000 up-and-coming writers nationwide.

Successful in continuing our aim of promoting writing and creativity in children, our regional anthologies give a vivid insight into the thoughts, emotions and experiences of today's younger generation, displaying their inventive writing in its originality.

The thought, effort, imagination and hard work put into each poem impressed us all and again the task of editing proved challenging due to the quality of entries received, but was nevertheless enjoyable. We hope you are as pleased as we are with the final selection and that you continue to enjoy *Future Voices From Wales* for many years to come.

CONTENTS

Louise Daly   1

Abersychan Comprehensive School
    Rebecca Filer   1
    Elliott Whiting   2
    Polly Harris   2
    Jacob Nash   3
    Lindsey Harbourne   4
    Hayley Teague   4
    Bethan Powell   5
    Robert Davies   6
    Michael Beacham   7
    Benjamin Harris   8
    Susie Kingdon   8
    Sarah Lamrick   9
    Sarah Smith   10
    Sian Arthur   10
    Michelle Richards   11
    Stephanie White   11
    Simon Dando   12
    Kylieanne Williams   12
    Christopher Powell   13
    Ian Roynon   14
    Christopher Booth   14
    Gareth Williams   15
    Leigh Watkins   16
    Carly Pearce   16
    Cian Woods   17
    Julia Broomhead   18
    Matthew Harris   19
    Chloe Driscoll   20

Atlantic College
    Neasa Coll   21

Bettws High School

Tara Dennen	22
Gareth Evans	22
Lianne Sheppard	23
Emily Galligan	24
Meryl Kemp	24
Leah Williams	25
Bethan Stacey	26
Kandice Murch	27
Beth Savage	28
Kathryn Reade	28
Casey Hooper	29
Charlene Ranford	30
Matthew Casey	30
Sophie Sellwood	31
Sarah Pocock	32
Tina Harley	32
Jamie Dudley	33
Lisa Kent	34
Katie Hayes	34
Emily Hillman	35
Kayleigh Jinks	36
Jennifer Evans	36
Rachel Hislop	37
Francesca Henderson	37
Samantha Bowden	38
Rebecca Chamberlain	38
Stacey Haynes	39
Sarah Caldweel-Kyle	39
Adele Croker	40
Alexander Mayne	40
Natalie Hughes	41
Michelle Jones	41
Jenna Lewis	42
Luke Embrey	42
Sarah Rees	43
Charlotte Cooper	43
Emma Chorley	44

Amy Cousins	44
Gemma Wainfur	45
Jemma Greenhaf	45
Emma Brown	46
Jessica Crumpler	46
Liz Short	47
Paul Davies	47
Kelly Bird	48
Kylie Murray	48
Becky Johnson	49
Ami Churcher	49
Charlotte Jennings	50
Lee-Ann Wellington	50
Jamie Smith	51
Adam Blake	51
Cathy Robins	52
Danielle Bolt	53
Leanne Pitman	54
Vicky Howells	55
Michael Walton	56
Jenna Travers	57
Rebecca Jones	58
Daniel Baiton	58
Matthew Fife	58
Michelle Price	59
Beth Savage	59
Kayleigh Cooper	59
Samantha Lilygreen	60
Natalie Willis	60
Laura Tuck	61
Lucy Marsh	62
Sara Millichip	63
James Shinton	64
Eleanor Venables	65
Simon Harvey	66
Melissa Arlett	67
Sîan Evans	68
Kirsty Wallis	68

Cyfartha High School

Elizabeth Church	69
Michael Thomas	69
Siân Burke	70
Bradley David	71
Rhian Elin James	72
Thomas Few	72
Thea Meek	73
Leanne Murphy	74
Nathan Wise	74
Siân Martin	75
Rebecca Moyles	76
Natasha Jones	76
Emma Burke	77
Hannah Taylor-Kensell	78
Jonathan Davies	79
Daniel Stickler	79
Lewis Bevan	80
Adam Ridley	80
Kristian James	81
Adam Jones	81

Llantwit Major Comprehensive School

Adam Wordley	82
Lindsay Kempley	82
Jon Jeffreys	83
Alex Branton	84
Lizzy Kelf	85
Lucy Edwards	86
Julia Williams	87
Laura Whitby	88
Will Ambrose	89
James Page	89
Samantha Roberts	90
Kim Sewell	91
Gemma Davies	92
James Norman	93

Mynyddbach Comprehensive School

Zoe James	94
Sarah Barry	95
Sammy Lewis	95
Lisa Davies	96
Natalie Lloyd	96
Ceri Williams	97
Sarah Collins	97
Katie Williams	98
Lisa Jones	98
Carly Thomas	99
Sarah Taylor	99
Amanda Palmer	100
Claire Evans	100
Helen Corbett	100

Pen-Y-Dre High School

Nerys Thomas	101
Kelly Hamer	101
Michael James	102
Sam Shipman	102
Linzy Phillips	103
David Kelly	104
Natalie Davies	106
Leearna Lyons	107
Lisa Hennessy	108
Rhiannon Meade	109
Marie Launchbury	110
Taryn Smale	111
Kelly Jones	112
Kylie Rees	113
Danielle Clark	114
Helen Jones	114
Amy Thomas	115
Adam Pollard	116
Lauren Bellshaw	116
Gavin Evans	117
Craig Beard	118

Natalie Jones	118
Sarah Farr	119
Rhiannon Evans	120
Kate Morgan	120
Adam Williams	121
Lynsey Murphy	122
Matthew Davies	122
Paula Hughes	123
Cerys Cook	124
Natalie Etheridge	124
Daniel Beattie	125
Adam James	126
Lyndsey Rogers	126
Elizabeth Johnson	127
Shane Small	128
Rhydian Patterson	128
Cheryl Evans	129
Taryn Rachel Evans	130
Stacey Price	130
Craig Baylis	131
Leanne Mew	131
Lee Bowditch	132
Jamie Lucas	132
Rebecca Jones	133
Lauran Brown	133
Hayley Jones	134
Christian Lewis	134
Katie Barrett	135
Scott David Thomas	135
Matthew Patrick	136
Gavin Williams	136
Jonathan Sims	137
Lyndsey Smith	137
Jennifer Price	138
Gareth French	138
Jenny Jones	139
Richard Jones	139
James Thomas	140

Kirstie James	140
Michael Williams	141
Rebecca Meade	142
Alex Morgans	143
Shalleena Mall	143
Charlotte Abraham	144
Denise Mahoney	144
Rhys Scrivens	145
Robert Phillips	146
Kirsty Purnell	147
Kelly Phillips & Kristie Abbruzzese	147
Carwyn Evans	148
Sian Lewis	148
Alex Davies	149
Anna Davies	149
Melanie Hier	150
Emma Kennedy	150
Laura Howley	151
David Jones	152
Leanne Hughes	153
Scott Vaughan	154
Caitlin McBride	155
Donna Williams	156
Simon Miles	157
Beth Rosser	157
Hannah Evans	158
Gemma Hughes	158
Nicky Jones	159
Lisa Marie Binks	160
Samantha Taylor	161
Kelly Thomas	162

Pontarddulais Comprehensive School

Simone Morris	163
Kaity Lee	163
Julie Anthony	164
Matthew Brooks	164
Robert Barnes	165

Laura Doidge	166
Rachael Flanagan	166
Zoe Charlotte Lewis	167
Sophie Lewis	168
Thomas Burgess	169
Emily Dawson	170
Emma Caie	171
Charlotte Sanders	172
Angharad Evans	173
Rachel Powell	174
Emma Morris	174
Linda Taylor	175
Angela Brugnoli	176
James Miles	176
Richard Price	177
Amber Carlisle	178
Alex Sutton	178
Lewis Evans	179
Jasmine Kelly	180
Vicki Erasmus	180
Rhodri Walters	181
Eluned Erasmus	182
Elinor Lewis	182
Linda Lewis	183
Joanne Richards	184
Joanne Sulsh	184
Natalie Adams	185
Claire Anne McEwan	186
Natasha Lewis	186
Stephen Drew	187
Victoria Davies	187
Stuart Edwards	188
Daniel Hurden	188
Sarah Wassell	189
Ceri Probert	190
Sam Batsford	190
Ashley Draisey	191
Natalie Thomas	192

Phillip White	192
Claire Gow	193
Amanda Robertson	194
Mark Jason Ford	194
Andrew Thomas	195
Sarah Phelps	195
Cara Jayne George	196
Adam Holley	196
Gemma Glenister	197
Catrin Brauner	198
Maryanne Temblett	198
Holly Vipond	199
Lauren Evans	200
Charlene Davies	200
Amy Davies	201
Ashley Lewis	202
Stuart Mindt	202
Kirsty Wilson	203
Sara Gwynne	204
Leanne John	204
Laura Williams	205
Cheryl Davies	205
Nathan Greenwood	206
James Frazer	206
Andrew Quinn	207
Lelly Leanne Hire	208
Dale Thomas	208
David Taylor	209
Thomas Reid	210
Louise Lisk	211
Matthew Fuge	212
Dario Fisher	213
James Freeman	214
Kirsty Evans	215
Christian Davies	216
Zoe Davison	216
Nicola Davidson	217
Nicholas Howells	217

Catherine Edwards	218
Charlotte Thomas	218
Carrie Gower	218
Christopher Day	219
Catrin Lloyd	219
Helene Rodde	220
Sarah Ann Tribe	220
Hannah Rödde	221
Robert Heycock	221
Natalie Sabido	222
Kirsty Roberts	222
Emma Black	223
Stacey Andrews	223
Rhys Francis	224
Rachel Berry	224
Alexander Hawken	225
Bethan Turner	225
Kelly Franks	226
Michelle Planck	226
James Beynon	227
Christopher Gardner	227
Laura Buckingham	228
Ruth McCarry	229
Nicola Cox	230
Claire Mainwaring	230
Kevin Davies	231
Johnathan Davies	231
Rachel Buckley	232
Kirsty Joseph	233
Kayleigh James	234
Danielle Rees	234
Paul Elliott	235
Ayat Tahir	235
Charlene Smith	236
David Carl Miles	237
Sarah Brown	238
Amy Kelly	238
Leyah Hillman	239

Sara Lloyd	239
Laura Harvey	240
Tom Williams	241
Natalie Wassell	242
Nicola Benson	242
Martin Nelson	243
Leanne Andrews	243
Rebecca Barton	244
Huma Pervez	245
Rhian Harris	246
Charlotte Button	246
Jemma O'Brien	247
Ben Matthews	247
Rhys Turner	248
Rachel Gibbon	249
Mark Phillips	250
Emma Louise Bolt	250
Nicola Hearne	251
Jamie Clement	251
Sharon-Louise Jones	252
Coralie Mouncher	253
Briony Ruth Frayne	254
Alistair Veck	255
Dylan Lewis	256
Sarah Richards	257
Jaimee Davies	258
Matthew Elvins	259
Bradleigh Brooks	260

Sir Thomas Picton School

Andrew Richards	261
Charlotte Morgan	261
Natalie Carol Mayhew	262
Paul Evans	263
Heather Coles-Riley	264
Laura Cornish	265
Bethan Phillips	266
Laura Clements	266

Becky Gau 267
Rachel Lewis 267
Sara-Jane Jones 268
Danielle Edwards 269
Barry Bowen 270
Christopher Strzelecki 270
Helen Bowden 270
Annie Slater 271
Arrun Shaw 272
Amanda Rayworth-Kiernan 272
Vincent Thorne 272
Verity Halls 273
Hannah Rastall 273
Sarah Nicholls 273
Hannah Evans 274
Kelly-Anne Davies 274
Luke Hughes 274
Rachel Horne 275
Simon Lewis 275
Gemma Jones 275
Eleanor Richards 276
Gemma Bevan 276
Sarah McPherson 276
Kim Dunlop 277
Samantha Bevan 277
Tom Chaloner 277
Amy Archer 278
Anne-Marie Bentley 278
Hayley Reeves 278
Alice Lewis 279

Ysgol Uwchradd Tregaron
Christopher Clare 279
Christina Gray 280
Jennifer Claire Davies 280
Carys Davies 281
Emyr Davies 282
Joseph Williams 282

Claire Davies 283
Emma Stevens 284
Caryl Davies 284
Joe Roberts 285
Catrin Jones 285
Peter Horton 286
Gwenan Arch 286
Mark Leese 287
Grace Acres 287
Daniel Williams 288
Robert Hockey 288
Rebecca Pugh 289
Laura Regan 290

The Poems

FRIENDSHIP POEM

My best friend does a lot for me,
She always makes me happy when I am sad,
My best friend is a good person.
Who hardly ever gets into trouble.
She is someone I can trust,
My best friend and I have lots of good times,
My best friend likes reading books, so do I.
We like riding together,
We both like playing on PlayStations,
We both like All Saints and B*witched.

Louise Daly (11)

SNOWMEN

They start from snow that has fallen on the ground,
They are made up to look fat and round.
They have a carrot for a nose with coal buttons and eyes,
They wear a scarf and a hat and can be any old size.
The body is where you start and to do that you need to
Roll up some snow from on the ground and stick it down
with imaginary glue.
Next there is the head and this is how you do it,
Roll up a ball of snow and stick it on with invisible Pritt.
Take an old hat and scarf and put it where it should be,
Then take some coal and add it to his face and tummy.
Take a carrot for his nose and some twigs for his arms
And snowballs for his hands, so he hasn't any palms.
All that's left to do is to choose a name,
So make sure that it has something to do with frozen rain.
And now all you have to do is to sit back and enjoy
And to decide in your mind whether it's a girl or a boy.

Rebecca Filer (11)
Abersychan Comprehensive School

THE RUGBY WORLD CUP

The Rugby World Cup has come to Wales
People are singing throughout the vales
The Welsh team are back on track
We've never had a stronger pack.

The very first game was under way
Wales and Argentina were first to play
Wales won the match fair and square
I had to go to school but I wish I was there.

The Millennium Stadium was full of supporters
Fathers, sons and even their daughters,
They were there cheering their team
Helping Wales fulfil their dream.

Welsh people singing throughout the vale
Come on Wales you cannot fail
The final will be a very special day
The World Cup is in Wales to stay.

Wales 23 Argentina 18.

Elliott Whiting (12)
Abersychan Comprehensive School

I THANK THE LORD I'M WELSH

'I thank the Lord I'm Welsh'
So many people say.
But do they really mean it,
What do you think, yea or nay?

They say they love the mountains
The grassy hills and lakes.
They say they love the valleys
But do they care for it?

Do they keep their rubbish
Or just throw it on the ground?
Do they care for monuments
Or just let them crumble to the floor?

'I thank the Lord I'm Welsh'
So many people say.
But do they really mean it,
What do they think, yea or nay?

Polly Harris (11)
Abersychan Comprehensive School

EARTH

Once were hills, valleys and trees,
But pollution and smoke brought green to its knees,
We tried to intervene,
We tried to stop,
But exhaust smoke and fumes still
Damage the crop.

We didn't mean to end the Earth,
Please don't go away,
Let's do our bit to keep it clean,
So it can breathe another day.

Stop the chop,
Save the trees,
Stop more cash for the billionaire sleaze
From London to Moscow,
Or Washington to Perth,
Please protect our beautiful little Earth.

Jacob Nash (15)
Abersychan Comprehensive School

WINTER!

In the bleak mid winter,
it is very cold
for the winds blow and howl.
The trees are bare
and there is a chill
from under the door.
The floorboards creak
and the rain splutters
against the ground.
The hail and snow
race down from the sky,
while children gather snow
ready to make a snowman.
Icicles hang from door to door
and frost lays on the window sills.
Melting snow on the pavement
and snowballs flying through the air.
Children sledging down the hill,
People skating on the lake,
It is definitely winter.

Lindsey Harbourne (11)
Abersychan Comprehensive School

SHOOTING STAR

As I look up to the ink blue sky
So many stars are stood alone
Then I see you in the distance
Could I? Can I fly with you?

You need no wings for you to fly
Across the lonely, still dark sky
There is no limit, where you can go
Could I? Can I fly with you?

So many stars, you pass night by
You do not need to gaze and stay
On a mysterious journey, you aim to go
Could I? Can I fly with you?

I need to know my shooting star
If I might travel on a journey too
Across the lonely, still dark sky
Could I? Can I fly with you?

Hayley Teague (15)
Abersychan Comprehensive School

SO LONG

All of these feelings,
I can't run and hide,
I want to know how you feel tonight,
All these feelings going down the drain,
Now I want to know why you put me through this pain,
Now I

Don't know,
I don't care,
If I told you, you won't care,
Oh no,
You don't care,
You didn't even say 'so long.'

Baby, bye, bye
Move on,
My love goes on,
I'll be strong
Because I know that I'm gonna get you one day.

Bethan Powell (14)
Abersychan Comprehensive School

RE-DE-EVOLUTION

What are we doing to ourselves?
Men are becoming women
And junkie's brains are swimming
Of thoughts of love and hate and war
Underneath their visions of Jesus, cigar smoking fish and the coming
from behind the door.
So where are we going
Why are our lives being lived for us
Why can't we break this incorruptible loop of human -
Re-De-Evolution
And all we're worried about is whether we've missed the last bus.

We're becoming obsessed with fluffy coffee, real people's TV and the
word etceteras
And we work and slave forty-eight weeks of the year
Just so we can have two weeks of being unhappy by the sand
And the music industry today is full of self-righteous pop bands
Who make us know what we want to hear.

So where are we going
Why are our lives being lived for us
Why can't we break this incorruptible loop of human -
Re-De-Evolution
And all we're worried about is whether we've missed the last bus.

Why do we remove skin from our noses and replace it with that from
our rears?
Why do we pull back our skin and shave behind our ears?
Why do we have alarm clocks chiming?
Why do I hate rhyming?
Why do we question ourselves?

So where are we going
Why are our lives being lived for us
Why can't we break this incorruptible loop of human -
Re-De-Evolution
And all we're worried about is whether we've missed the last bus.

Robert Davies (14)
Abersychan Comprehensive School

THE NOAH RAP

Yo, my name is Noah
I'm the coolest dude around
I live in Israel
And I'm not popular with the crowd.

One night I was asleep
When God spoke to me
He said, 'Build me an ark to put on the sea'
So I worked and worked as fast as I could and
chopped down all the necessary wood.

The rain came down
The floods went up
The waves grew bigger
And we all began to shiver.

I sent one bird
It didn't come back
So I sent one more
And it flew back.

We knew it was safe
So we started to unload
We all lived together
And we happily grew old.

Michael Beacham (12)
Abersychan Comprehensive School

WE DON'T NEED NO EDUCATION (PINK FLOYD)

Baseline profiles must improve,
this child has got to move, move, move!
Attainment targets have been set,
they must at all costs, at least, be met.

In your past glory you shall not bask,
you haven't done this reading task.
You'll work, work, work, so don't be dumb,
follow the National Curriculum!

Exam boards want this - so forget about yourself,
read those guidelines on the shelf.
You're only achieving level 4,
can't you work properly anymore?

You must do better in your SATs
and don't you dare forget your CATs.
Fail GCSEs? Don't be absurd,
that would be the end of the world.

Tests and exams - more and more,
make us crash out on the floor!
All this talk of NFER,
are statistics all kids are?

Benjamin Harris (14)
Abersychan Comprehensive School

THE ART ROOM

An artist's pallet of colours fills the room
A step into a fantasy
Patchwork walls with samples of patterns
Eyes watching from every angle
Faces of sadness, faces of joy
Portraits tell their own story.

Hear the swish of brushes in water pots
Swirling like a whirlpool
Chalk to board and pencil to paper
Sense the concentration of those who work
Images of ideas racing through their heads
The aroma of drying paint lingers in the room
Inhaling masterpieces painted with emotion.

Susie Kingdon (14)
Abersychan Comprehensive School

THE BEACH

As I walk along the fragile, grainy sand,
The waves close in with their everlasting tirade.
The fresh scent of salty sea air leaves me
breathless.
While the blazing yellow face of the sun smiles upon me.
A gust of blowing wind hauls me back,
I hear scuttling crabs in their sideways race
And as my feet crunch on bloodshot shells,
I hear the screeching seagulls scavenging the shoreline,
Swooping sharp talons ready to devour.
I dive into the ocean,
I feel the cold sharp fingers stab my body.
The slothful sand slowly surrounds my feet,
I see a whirlpool of fish titillated by the rhythmic
Movement of the waves.
Now I sit, wet on a gluey cushion of sand.
I bite into my sandy sandwich.
Amongst other things I taste gritty sand
And a sharp burst of salt lingers on my tongue,
As the majestic colours of the sunset blend to make one.

Sarah Lamrick (13)
Abersychan Comprehensive School

FLY THE WINGS OF AN EAGLE

Fly the wings of an eagle
Over hills and valleys
Under clouds and bridges
Through warm summer air
And cold chilling winter winds.

You stand high upon a rock you see your scuttling prey
Its tiny legs scampering away from your sharp claw.

You swoop down low to catch your prey
Then glide and swoop back to your rock
Where you gulp and swallow
Your tasty meaty prey
You look your best with your gracious wings
So that's why I wish, I could
Fly the wings of an eagle.

Sarah Smith (12)
Abersychan Comprehensive School

BLUE

Blue is the solitude that surrounds me;
The corners of my fears.

Blue is the cold hands of my past, clinging on to me
And the looming presence of the future.

Blue is the walls of my life closing in on me
But also the vast stretch of nothingness before me.

Blue is the words that I am afraid to write,
The thoughts that I am afraid to think
And blue is myself.

Sian Arthur (15)
Abersychan Comprehensive School

SOMETIMES

Sometimes I run, into a dark corner to
think of what's going on in the world.
Sometimes I look around and I see some
people hurt, tired, hungry and poor.
Sometimes I read to see people without homes
and their family.
Sometimes I eat and think how lucky I am
to have a cooked dinner every Sunday.
Sometimes I say 'Christmas' and then think
that some people have no presents or Christmas
dinner, they just sit there sad and lonely.
Sometimes I feel the soft warm bed and to
think other people are just in cardboard
boxes, on the streets and nowhere to go.
Sometimes I just think how lucky I am . . .

Michelle Richards (11)
Abersychan Comprehensive School

IMAGINE

I close my eyes and imagine the things I like
to see, a great blue sky, the green, green grass.
That's the way the world should be.
A soft white kitten tight as a ball on the
rug in front of the fire. A warm, bright glow
filling a gloomy room.

I imagine a tree, a lonely tree on the top of
a hill swaying with the wind, blowing through
the leaves. A little boy smiling, playing with
a toy train, that's what I imagine when I close my eyes.

Stephanie White (11)
Abersychan Comprehensive School

SUMMER'S GONE

This is a path I've walked a million times
This is a day I've lived before
But I don't want it to end
And I don't want it to leave.
Summer's gone and it's not coming back
The leaves are falling off the trees
It's freezing cold out here
Where's the summer gone?
I'm sick of frost already
It's only been a day
I want it to end
Now it's pouring with rain.
Summer's gone and it's not coming back
The leaves are falling off the trees
It's freezing cold out here
Where's the summer gone?

Simon Dando (12)
Abersychan Comprehensive School

BLUE MOON

The blue moon
Shines night after night
And everyone likes
Its glorious light.

When the stars
Come out to play
The sun will come
And put them away.

When the blue moon's
Curtains are drawn,
The sun starts rising
To tell you it's dawn.

Kylieanne Williams (13)
Abersychan Comprehensive School

IN THE SUPERMARKET

I smell
Fresh fruit
Colourful red fresh meat
The smell of freshly baked bread.

I touch
The cold sharp trolley
The soft cold fridges
The smooth cylindrical rails.

I hear
The sound of the squeaking wheel of the trolley
The people talking,
Tills pinging open.

I taste
The taste of freshly baked bread
Fresh fruit and veg
And perfume mixed together.

I see
Money mixing
Children singing
Lovely food with decorations
Bright lights and signs.

Christopher Powell (14)
Abersychan Comprehensive School

DON'T LET THE SUN GO DOWN ON ME

The sun was sinking into the ocean
as I glanced up at it,
the dazzling rays hit the waves,
as it sunk cautiously beneath the sea.
The half-eaten sun was radiant
as it slithered piece by piece further beneath the waves,
the orange sky was getting darker
while it was losing the conflict.
The last beam of light crept out
from below the sea.
It took one solitary gasp for air
as the closing blow was struck.
The orange sky abruptly faded
and a jet-black sky arose
from the ashes of the battle,
the darkness had won but for how long?

Ian Roynon (14)
Abersychan Comprehensive School

WORLD IN UNION

In this rugby World Cup and all of its mothers,
This song is sung like no single other.
Fans sing with togetherness, the world as a whole,
Even every player sings, every person, every soul.

If only it was like that because even as we speak,
The future of our world seems so drear and very bleak,
Cos all around the world, wars are breaking out,
Look at Northern Ireland or Kosovo, if only we could
have a shout.

If all the people from every race
Gathered together in one single place
Whether it's the sports of football, cricket or rugby,
Brings the whole world together in harmony!

Christopher Booth (12)
Abersychan Comprehensive School

THE GYM

As you walk through doors,
Of giant proportion,
They slam behind, locking you in.
With every caution,
You tiptoe on,
For this beast of a hall has taken you in.
The smell of sweat,
Lashes out at your nose.
Its salty, bitter aroma,
Clings to your throat,
Tickling your tastebuds.
It makes you cough.
As the class before leaves,
In time for the next storm to arrive.
They clamber up the rough,
Bear fur thread as it wiggles,
Through their hands and feet.
Each hair probes deep into the skin.
Next comes the old wooden frame.
Each knot, scrape, dent and grain,
Runs across your fingers.
Now that the lesson's over,
You slide across the shiny floor,
Towards the door again.

Gareth Williams (14)
Abersychan Comprehensive School

DANCING QUEEN

She dances so elegantly
In the coldness of the air
Her body moves from side to side
And the wind blows her hair.
She dances like no one
I've ever seen before,
She glides through the air like an eagle
You could never ignore.
How is she so talented?
Could she be real?
Her body flows within the wind
From her forehead to her heel.
So that is why they all call her
The Dancing Queen.

Leigh Watkins (11)
Abersychan Comprehensive School

WATER

It whirls and swirls in twists of blue.
Blue, white all different colours, many shapes too.
It splashes on the cliff surface,
violently, crashing, doing back flips
off the high rock,
tumbling down urgently.
It pours from the sky,
sometimes acid poison that destroys the forests,
or sometimes floating down angelically refreshing,
thirsty plants and flowers.
Everyone has a daily use for water,
water is everywhere.

Carly Pearce (14)
Abersychan Comprehensive School

THE SWIMMING POOL

I hear . . .
People splashing in the sparkling
Deep blue water.
People shouting and screaming.
The water bubbling
The wall echoing as if they're trying to reply back to you.

I touch . . .
The smooth cold
Tiles, the cold smooth
Ladders to climb the
Gritty walls.

I smell . . .
The sweet
Fresh air.

I taste . . .
The tangy taste
Of chlorine it tasted
Like a red coated
Plum ripened freshly picked.

I see . . .
The lively people
Splashing in the pool
Like a salmon springing
Up through water.
The people diving into the pool
As when a rock hits water.

Cian Woods (14)
Abersychan Comprehensive School

FIREWORKS

Everyone gathers around to see,
the bright fireworks, loud as can be.
Shooting up, never to stop, then you hear a pop.
Droplets of colour floating down,
almost but not, hitting the ground.

Children shouting, excited to see,
wide open eyes, hard to believe.
Jumping and squealing happy as can be
different colours like they've never seen.

Blue and green I could see
a touch of red
almost falling on me.
I ran, moved away, into a crowd. Trying to
get away from the sound.

A big loud squeal like I've never heard
again, again.
Two loud pops then a loud bang
colours spill out, what a beautiful one.

A roll of drums, then a swirl
a Catherine wheel
in a golden curl.
I've never heard fireworks so loud
loud enough to deafen the crowd.

Julia Broomhead (15)
Abersychan Comprehensive School

THE BLUE LAGOON

The sound of splashing emanates,
From a building painted white as snow,
The sound of laughter,
The sound of joy,
Makes the entire place glow.
The smell of chlorine hits you,
Like a twenty-foot truck,
The brightness of the water astounds you
And invites you into a blue lagoon.
Standing timidly on the edge,
Like a first day back at school,
The shimmering shining water,
Looking up at you.
I reluctantly take the plunge,
Into the blue unknown,
But soon it will be the colour red,
I am to behold.
The chlorine irritates my eyes,
With the burning rage of the sun,
It's the battle every swimmer fights,
Never to be won.
Finally our session expires,
With our fingers shrivelled like prunes,
We dry our exhausted bodies
And comb our seaweed hair.

Matthew Harris (13)
Abersychan Comprehensive School

THE STABLES

The sickly smell of dung fills the air,
Along with the sweet scent of hay and sawdust,
The polished leather saddles in the tack room,
Shine like the sun.
Bringing shame to the muddy bridles.

The horses kick the doors
With their shod hooves
And snort impatiently.
Their coats are sleek,
Their bodies warm
I can hear them munching their food
Making a noise like a steam
Train's pistons.

As I enter the stables to
Brush the horses tangled manes
And scruffy tails,
I taste this morning's cornflakes
Mixed with the rancid stench of
Wet sawdust.

When I've done my jobs
I leave the dirty, smelly stables
And return
To the *clean mess*
That is home.

Chloe Driscoll (13)
Abersychan Comprehensive School

EDGES

You're too young to be dying
in your own skin
I'm reading your tattoos like history books
diseases showing from within.

Because the edges are blurring
between what's worth it
and what's not
and the edge is always closer
when you're all you've got.

The doctors are all talking
naming numbered pills
I'm tearing into waiting room chairs
I know they're counting silent kills.

Because I know that
half this world grows up too fast
while the other half is laughing
half this world breaks free from chains
and half locks them up again.

We're left chasing the sun
to burn the edges in.

Neasa Coll (17)
Atlantic College

FEELINGS

Feelings - sad, happy, proud, hurt,
Who wants feelings anyway?
No one likes to be sad
And no one likes to be offended.

Feelings come, feelings go
I wish we never had them,
Feelings make things worse.
First you're sad, then you're sunk.

But feelings are also happy,
Which most people prefer.
We wouldn't appreciate anything
If feelings were not here.

Being proud, being happy
And feeling like you're wanted.
We all want these things
And these are all feelings.

So feelings are confusing
Yet feelings make us confused,
But if we never had them,
Then life would be like symmetry.

Tara Deneen (13)
Bettws High School

A BOY

There was a boy
Who wanted to be a cowboy,
In two years' time he wanted to play, really boys,
Like two cowboys.
He worked on a farm
Which was greatly unarmed.
He played cowboys in a band.

But there was a story,
Like a poorly lady
Who lived in a hay stack,
Who frightened the boy away,
The boy ran away up the mountain far away,
The lady took control and went the right way.

Gareth Evans
Bettws High School

THE MYSTERY TRIP

I walked to school with aching feet
And it was such a dull day,
My teacher said we had a surprise,
A trip for a day away.

What was this trip? I wondered,
As I went from class to class,
Would it be a big adventure
Or just more field trips in green grass?

The day of the trip came,
The weather was fine, hooray,
At least we wouldn't get wet,
The coach came late, not again.

We drove for quite a while,
Along the motorway and past hills,
When we stopped after nearly two hours,
The surprise was really a thrill.

An adventure park, wow! Great!
We went on all the rides,
Water rapids, Twister and Devil's Temple,
What a day to remember.

Lianne Sheppard
Bettws High School

IT'S MY LIFE

Why, Mum, did you run away
And leave me all alone?
Now there is an ache inside me
And I cannot let it go.
Come back Mum.

I now know the burden you were under,
The strain that we had caused,
The demands that we made,
But we could have made it better
If you'd told us, we would have listened
And you would have stayed.
Come back Mum.

I miss you,
Dad misses you,
Kev misses you,
He doesn't understand why you left,
He thinks you'll come back soon,
But you won't.
These tears he cries for you will never wipe away,
Till you come home, Mum.
Life will never be the same.
Come back Mum.

Emily Galligan (13)
Bettws High School

THE BRIGHT BLUE SKY

The bright blue sky above us all
Sitting calmly and beautiful,
Light and wonderful or dark and grey,
The sun that sits with golden ray.

The skies that look evil, with thunder and lightning,
Thunder and lightning, which is very; very frightening,
Rain is now coming with so much force,
People below know it will have to take its course.

Meryl Kemp (11)
Bettws High School

MR MILES

My teacher Mr Miles,
Never ever smiles.
He has a big nose
And out of it hair grows.
He wears a wig,
His ears are big.
He looks a century old,
He's started growing mould.
He really is old fashioned,
He still thinks food is rationed.
He wants to bring back the cane,
I think he's insane.
He has a cold stare
That gives us quite a scare.
He thinks nasty thoughts,
Has a wrinkled face with warts.
If some trouble occurs,
Steam comes from his ears.
He's as small as an elf,
He can't even reach the shelf.
I wish we had a normal teacher
Instead of this wild creature.

Leah Williams
Bettws High School

SUPPOSE

Suppose I was a princess
With a palace made of gold,
I'd have servants, maids and butlers
To wait on me alone.

Suppose I was a popstar,
Singing in a famous band,
We'd tour around the country
And be known throughout the land.

Suppose I was an astronaut,
Flying to the moon,
I'd wave goodbye to my family
And say, 'I'll be back soon.'

Suppose I was a millionaire
With money to throw away,
I'd buy everything I wanted
And invite all my friends to stay.

Suppose I was a teacher,
Bossing children around,
I'd make them listen to me,
There wouldn't be a sound.

Suppose I was a spider
With the biggest web you've ever seen,
I'd catch bugs, flies and insects,
I'd be really, really mean.

Suppose I was a dancer,
performing on a stage,
I'd have costumes by the dozen,
My outfits would be all the rage.

Oh how I hope I'm never these things,
Cos I'd just rather be me.

Bethan Stacey (12)
Bettws High School

THERE'S THIS LITTLE GIRL!

There's this little girl with scraggy hair,
Big, big feet like a polar bear!
Captivating demon eyes
With a jelly face and thunder thighs.
A pointed, ugly, devil chin,
She skips around with a dusty bin.
A squashed and disfigured ugly nose,
Out of it long hair gruesomely grows.
She never, ever scrubs her teeth,
She always picks at them underneath.
Never, no never, washes her locks,
It looks like seaweed from the docks.
She has skinny, thin, knobbly knees,
She tries to play footie, but there's no skill,
She thinks she's cool, she thinks she's brill,
She's so ugly and so unpretty,
She's the ugliest in the whole city.
There's only one thing I have to say,
Why is she so abnormal in this way?
I will now keep myself to myself,
I'm quite ugly, I'm an elf!

Kandice Murch (13)
Bettws High School

A POEM ABOUT A POEM

People tell you all the time
Poems do not have to rhyme,
It's often better if they don't,
And that is why this one won't.
(Ooops!)
There's ballad, nonsense, ode and limerick,
Narrative, sonnet, riddle and acrostic,
To write poetry is very hard,
Especially trying to write a ballad.
(Ooops, I've done it again!)
There's simile, metaphor and personification,
Verse, stanza and alliteration,
My favourite is simile, it goes like this ;-
The chips were as soggy as a wet granny's kiss.
(Ooops, and again!)
There's Shelly, Byron, Keats and Wordsworth,
Donne, Morrel, Blake and Shakespeare,
All of these writers are very famous
For writing poetry which does not rhyme.
(Hurray, hurray!)

Beth Savage (12)
Bettws High School

JAN'S DESPAIR

A heavy weight lies on my shoulders,
Day after day after day,
But the greening hills and the fresh cool breeze
Make me see things a different way.

The sick feeling goes and I'm happy,
Remembering the good times I had,
But then I suddenly remember
How she hurt me, Kevin and Dad.

My mind is a whirl of emotions,
Confused, happy and sad,
I miss her, love her, hate her,
Because she's treated me bad.

I see the difference between the bad and the good
And the changes in my life,
But all I want is for her to come home,
And be a loving mother and wife.

Kathryn Reade (14)
Bettws High School

THE DAY I WAS BORN

On the day I was born the birds chirped
On the day I was born an old man jumped
On the day I was born clocks stopped
On the day I was born an army fought
On the day I was born the sun beamed
On the day I was born the stars shone
On the day I was born bells rang
On the day I was born the sea splashed
On the day I was born politicians rose
On the day I was born planets dropped
On the day I was born choirs sang
On the day I was born bullies froze
On the day I was born vicars shouted
On the day I was born doctors clapped
On the day I was born clothes fashioned
On the day I was born the elderly spoke
On the day I was born the young became polite
On the day I was born schools became fun
On the day I was born life . . . changed.

Casey Hooper
Bettws High School

IT'S MY LIFE - WHERE IS SHE?

Where is she?
She's been gone for so long,
Left us all alone.

Everyone wants to help,
But that won't bring her back.
It's like a dark tunnel
With no end.

When I look around, all I see is faces,
Watching, waiting, gossiping.

It's like nothing is real,
Nothing can be felt,
Except a deep ache inside me.

It's a misery I can't name,
It gets darker
And still no end.
Where is she?

Charlene Ranford (14)
Bettws High School

CARDS

Red, black, Queens and Jacks,
Three, four, seven and more,
Ace, Queens, Kings and Jacks,
Are the faces of the pack.

In your hand a magic trick,
It's not real, but it's so quick.
Sets of cards are not just numbers,
They're just there to make you wonder.

A game of Pairs, a game of Snap,
And a game of Rummy out the back,
A few friends around the table,
Paul, Mark, Matthew and Mabel.

Tricks, faces, numbers and more,
Is what you need for heaven galore,
Just some places and you will see,
A pack of cards is the key.

Matthew Casey (11)
Bettws High School

I AM THE BULLY

I am the bully!
I live in every school, every playground,
I have been around for a very long time,
I go to every school, every school where
Little children are scared of me,
My families are people who frighten other people,
Who make people feel unwanted.
I have got many friends,
Friends that agree with everything I say and do as I say,
I like making people feel unwanted,
Deserted, lonely,
I come from everywhere, I rule everything,
I am always there watching someone,
You can find me not far away from someone
Who is crying, hurt.
You will never find me but I will find you,
I like it here, I rule everything,
Everything.
I am the bully!

Sophie Sellwood
Bettws High School

WHY CAN'T I?

Why can't I . . .
Be popular,
Pull people's hair,
Get told off
And never care?

Why can't I . . .
Be nice and kind
And pleasant,
No grief or sorrow?

Why can't I . . .
Live with people that care,
Have a dad with hair,
A teacher that's fair,
Why am I always . . .
Plain Sare?

(Sare - short for Sarah)

Sarah Pocock (12)
Bettws High School

AT THE BOTTOM OF MY GARDEN

Golden, yellow daffodils
Swaying in the breeze,
Like dancing little fairies
At the bottom of my garden.

Scurrying little squirrels,
Rushing round collecting nuts,
For winter's round the corner
At the bottom of my garden.

Last leaves falling from the tree,
Scattered all over the ground,
Covering it like a carpet,
At the bottom of my garden.

Naked trees clothed with snow,
Like a big woolly jumper,
Not one branch bare,
At the bottom of my garden.

Tina Harley (13)
Bettws High School

CYMRAEG '99

The Rugby World Cup is under way
And our Welsh dragons are here to stay
They may be battered, they may be bruised
But they're defiant and they won't lose
With Rob Howley and the team
They'll be winners and reign
Supreme
We've beat the Argies and
the Japs
But against the Samoans we did collapse
The Aussies are the next in line
If we beat them we're doing fine
The semi-finals would be nice
But if we lose we'll pay the price
The final would be sheer delight
At the end of the tunnel there will be light
But win or lose, Wales don't despair
Because our Welsh pride will always be there!

Jamie Dudley (12)
Bettws High School

IT'S MY LIFE, I'M SORRY

I left so suddenly, but I know not why,
Just now I can see Kev, so stubborn, cry.
I didn't leave a note and I didn't say goodbye,
Now I know I've hurt them, I'm the one to cry.
But life was so boring, washing dishes every day,
Make the meal and hoover, they had nothing much to say.
How I wish I could see Jan's sweet, dazzling smile,
She always had admirers, the list went on a mile.
So many things Kev wanted, but he couldn't have to hold,
Now all he wants is me back, but my love for him's turned cold.
Life was just so boring, washing dishes every day,
Nothing new ever happened, nothing new to say,
Kev just watched the TV, Dad just wanted beer,
I think of Jan, left alone, because I'm no longer here.
I'm now somewhere happy, it's not just them, for now
To them my disappearance is wrong, they wonder why and how.
I know they're sad and lonely, and that anger burns inside,
I'm sorry Jan, Dad and Kev, my love for life has died.

Lisa Kent (13)
Bettws High School

I'M SORRY

I'm sorry for breaking a promise,
I'm sorry for doing things wrong,
I'm sorry for trying to make it right,
Because even that went wrong.

I'm sorry for not doing things right,
I'm sorry for making things wrong,
I know you'll always love me,
Whether I'm right or wrong.

I said I never do things wrong,
I said that and I was wrong,
I'm the one who's in the wrong,
It can't be you, because I'll be wrong.

You hate me and I hate you,
that's one thing that can't be true,
You love me and I love you,
That's one thing which will always be true.

Katie Hayes (14)
Bettws High School

LOVE AND HATE

Why me?
Why now?
Did it have to be?
Why did she go?
Why didn't she leave a note
To say when she was coming home?
I miss her so much,
But then I feel hate and anger.
Why hasn't she phoned
Or left a message,
Anything to stop me worrying?
We used to be one big, happy family,
But it has all been shattered.
I try to think what life would be like,
Jan Kev and I,
Me being the dad and mum,
I'm so scared.
How am I going to cope?

Emily Hillman (13)
Bettws High School

HALLOWE'EN

Hallowe'en
It's my favourite night,
Best time of the year
For giving people a fright.

Dressing up like monsters
Making people scream,
Trick or treating on people's doors
It's just like a bad dream!

Going to a Hallowe'en disco,
Doing the monster bash,
Throwing eggs at people
That land with an almighty smash!

So, am I sure you will see
A Hallowe'en party is the place to be,
Having fun on that spooky night
Giving friends a Hallowe'en fright.

Kayleigh Jinks
Bettws High School

AUNTIE JANE

Auntie Jane,
Has a big pain right at the side of her nose
And every morning without warning it very nearly glows.

She has long blonde hair that she styles with flair
And lips of a ruby red.

She's a bit strange my Auntie Jane
Because she spends all day in the shed!

Jennifer Evans (11)
Bettws High School

THE SEA

I walked along the beach,
Gazing out across the sea,
Stepping through the waves,
I heard a voice calling me.

I dived into the water
And swam down under the sea,
I saw the mermaid coming,
Her soft voice calling me.

We swam deep down together,
Greeting fish under the sea,
She started collecting pearls
And said, 'Help me, please' to me.

We collected pearls all day,
Then swam back up through the sea,
I was back up on the beach,
I heard her voice thanking me.

Rachel Hislop
Bettws High School

I AM A VICTIM

I am a victim a terrible scandal
I am burning inside like a candle
I feel like I am melting like the wax around it.
My only friend is a stuffed chicken
I have no friends in the whole world
I have only my family
But I can't build up the courage to tell them what is happening
I feel like I am the prey of a big eagle taking control of the sky.

Francesca Henderson (12)
Bettws High School

THE MAGICAL DRAGON

There once was a magical dragon
Who lived in the village of Smagon.
No one dared to enter
His cave of wonder,
The magical dragon of Smagon.

There once was a magical dragon
Who set a wonderful spell on St Magon.
He turned to a fish
And was eaten in a dish.
St Magon who got eaten by the dragon.

There once was a magical dragon
Who scared all the people of Smagon,
They never returned,
For their village was burned,
The magical dragon of Smagon.

Samantha Bowden
Bettws High School

I AM A VICTIM

I am a frightened little deer.
I come from a mountain not so far away,
I like grass which is as soft as me.
My friends are as frightened as me,
My enemies are cowardly wolves.
I'm happy when the cowardly wolves leave me alone.
It makes me sad when they torture me,
If I could change something, I would change
The bullies to be friendly people.
I'd get somebody to sort them out and change them.

Rebecca Chamberlain (12)
Bettws High School

WHAT IF?

What if the sky should fall?
What if I was a 100 feet tall?

What if I could fly like a kite?
What if I had great human might?

What if there was no more war?
What if no one was poor?

What if I was a Barbie girl?
What if I owned an oyster pearl?

What if I had a witches hand?
What if we lived in a beautiful land?
What if I was queen Cleopatra lying just getting fanned?

When I think of these things my eye slightly gleams
But really they're just dreams.

Stacey Haynes (12)
Bettws High School

THE BEACH

Yellow golden sand is shining
the blue sea shimmering
dolphins leaping high
crabs crawling
beach
crabs crawling
dolphins leaping high
the blue sea shimmering
yellow golden sand is shining.

Sarah Caldwell-Kyle (13)
Bettws High School

MY NAN

I love my nan,
She gives me money,
She gives me sweets,
Oh how I love my nan.

I love my nan,
She gives me tips,
Tells me jokes,
Oh, how corny they are!

I love my nan,
She takes me out,
Gives me treats,
Oh, how lucky I am!

Because after all without her, I'd be
Broke and never have my way!

Adele Croker (13)
Bettws High School

THE HAPPY MIRACLE

I saw my sister in the air,
She was coming down a flight of stairs,
I held out my hand and smiled with glee,
She held my hand and followed me.
Then she showed me Elvis Presley,
Then he sang for my mum and made her happy.
She said, 'It's time I went . . .'

I still remember it now rocking back and forth in my chair.

Alexander Mayne
Bettws High School

TEENAGE RELATIONSHIPS

Jan felt shocked.
Why would he ask her out?
She felt confused,
Why?
She felt embarrassed,
She blushed,
She said 'Hello.'
They sat down to talk
Over a cup of coffee.
They were talking
When she said 'No!'
In a sharp voice, to prove
She wasn't playing hard to get.
She was shy,
But she didn't know why.
She had known Pete for three years.

Natalie Hughes (13)
Bettws High School

LOOP DE LOOP

Let's fly kites,
From great heights,
Watch them swoop down then loop de loop,
Let them soar in the sky, let them fly, fly, fly,
With our heads held high,
We will watch them fly by,
With the wind in their tails,
We follow their trails,
Until they come to rest,
Then we discussed who flew best.

Michelle Jones (11)
Bettws High School

SCHOOL AND ME

My name is Jenna,
I'm 12 years old,
I look old for my age,
Or so I've been told,
I go to a school
Called Bettws High,
I'm quite good at my work,
'Cause I always try,
The head of my year is called Mrs Mere,
If you get into trouble, you gotta go see her,
'A detention for you,' she'll scream and she'll shout,
But I suppose that's better than a smack or a clout,
Shirts tucked in and no make-up for school,
But I think that's a silly rule,
As wearing make-up looks much more cool,
And shirts tucked in make you look a fool.

Jenna Lewis (12)
Bettws High School

THE WAR

1999, it was a nice day.
1939, it was a killing day.
Bombs dropping,
Guns shooting,
People dying,
Tanks destroying,
Houses falling,
Planes shooting,
Planes falling,
People screaming,
The sound is so loud!

Luke Embrey (12)
Bettws High School

WHY ME?

I don't feel as if I'm the same person,
I feel angry, fed-up and annoyed,
But yet I feel happier that my mum is safe.
I think a lot about where she might be,
I do miss her dreadfully.

I don't think my brother quite knows what is going on,
Maybe he does, but he's keeping himself to himself.
When I come home from school,
Everything seems to have changed.
I know I'm not going home to my mum.

When I saw the detective I was worried.
When he said he found a body in the lake
My heart and stomach left my body
And when he said he saw a young man with her,
I wondered who it might be.

Sarah Rees (14)
Bettws High School

GRANDAD

My grandad was a marvellous man,
He served his country and married my nan.
I loved him so, he was so sweet,
He was short and bald and had big feet.
I knew he loved me, you could see it in his eyes
And then one day he died.
My nan was very sad, everyone wept,
Everyone broke down into a heap.
He will be remembered in everyone's heart,
My grandad, my friend, my hero.

Charlotte Cooper (14)
Bettws High School

I JUST WANT LOVE

Love is so wonderful,
As you can see,
It's just like a diamond
Lying on a shelf
Every time I look.
It's always on my mind,
I just can't stop thinking,
Will I ever be loved?
I just want to be loved
Like a beautiful princess,
But days go by,
Nothing is found.
I just can't stop thinking
Will I ever be loved?

Emma Chorley (13)
Bettws High School

I AM A BULLY

I am as hard as a big bull,
I come from a place full of hard-faced bulls,
I like eating nuts because they're as hard as me.
My friends are as hard as me and the
People who pay me a bob a week,
My enemies are the little worms
In the corner of the yard.
I am happy when I'm beating up the little sheep,
Nothing makes me sad
Because I'm so mad.
If I could change anything,
I would be just a little softer.

Amy Cousins (12)
Bettws High School

ON MY BIKE

Pedalling hard up the hill,
Feeling sleepy and a bit ill,
Up I go,
All so slow,
I'm near the top,
I had better not stop,
Whee . . . down the hill I go,
Not at all slow,
A whistling sound in my ear,
It's the wind that I hear,
The trees go by all so fast,
It's like whizzing back to the past.
My heart's pumping,
My pulse is thumping,
With a big smile on my face,
Now I have won the race!

Gemma Wainfur (12)
Bettws High School

TIGERS

The tiger is a cat,
The tiger is a tree,
The tiger is a member of the cat family.

The tiger hunts his prey
Each and every day.

The paw prints in the jungle lead to the trees,
The tiger is climbing, eating leaves.
The tiger is pouncing after the deer,
Down his spine comes lots of fear.

Jemma Greenhaf
Bettws High School

Thoughts Of A Victim

I was walking down the road when,
Something hard like a rock hit me
on the face
then in the stomach,
again and again.
I never thought it would stop,
as I picked myself up off the floor.
Slowly dragging myself home,
I could still feel the pain,
rushing round my body
like a dozen pins pricking me,
all at once.
I can't stop this beast,
But someone will soon,
But until then I will always feel this pain.

Emma Brown (13)
Bettws High School

Autumn

Bare trees, stripped of their leaves,
Which lie on the floor like a red and gold carpet,
Evergreens mock their exposed wooden skeletons,
Waving their indestructible green branches
In the bitter cold air,
Birds soar away to warmer countries,
In a last attempt to escape
From the autumn atmosphere,
The sun sets as the final few birds
Wing their way south,
There they will stay until spring emerges
From winter's dense black heart.

Jessica Crumpler (12)
Bettws High School

I'M SORRY THAT I LEFT YOU

I really should have stayed at home
and tried to talk it through,
but now I'm sitting on this train,
What good does running do?
I don't know why I'm leaving home
I have done nothing wrong,
but now the train is moving on,
to them I am long gone.
I think of them by dead of night
tears brimming in my eyes,,
but leaving home I get away
from arguments and lies.
I sit here every day and night
with tears upon my cheek,
without you kids and even Dad,
my life is not complete.

Liz Short (13)
Bettws High School

THE DINOSAURS

Dinosaurs roamed the Earth millions of years ago.
In dust filled caves something moves, what is it?
No, could it be the dinosaur to wander the Earth.
Oh it is a Nothosaurus, what will it eat, fish or what?
So the first dinosaur to wander the Earth, what a wonder!
As this age goes on, food grows bleak, what can they eat?
Unexplainable nobody knows what gave dinos life.
Really we think we know what killed the great beast.
So ends a great era in the Earth's history but who
Knows they may come back one day or century?

Paul Davies (13)
Bettws High School

WHAT A LAUGH

I hate it,
I don't like it,
Wherever I go,
Whatever I do,
There they are,
Taking the mick,
Talking about me,
Laughing at me.

Every day they do it,
Laugh and joke about,
Nobody tells me,
Nobody warns me
About my skirt being tucked into my tights.

Kelly Bird
Bettws High School

FROM THE EYE OF A VICTIM

As I walk into a dark nightmare,
A rough paw on my shoulder.
As I turn to meet the beast again,
My heart beating like a drum,
My knuckles tightly clenched together.
Then with one punch,
The pain that screamed out.
Ten screams of pain,
All towards my face and stomach.
No one to stop this wild vulture,
Just one more cry from a pet for his collection.
One day this beast will meet his match,
To feel the pain, the cry and screams.

Kylie Murray (12)
Bettws High School

MIDNIGHT PALS

The silver moon is out at last and the sky is all but dark,
Suddenly I hear a padding sound just inside the park.
There it goes - a magnificent fox looking for bits of food,
Then I threw a bit of bread and thankfully he chewed.
When I got back I lay awake thinking about the fox.
Tomorrow night I'll go back out to see what else I'll spot.

The stars are shining brightly - I couldn't keep inside
Then swooped down an owl - how graceful is the glide.
A hedgehog came out from a bush and rolled up in a ball,
Then it rolled back out again and slowly it did crawl.
If you are out of bed at night, all you boys and gals,
Please look out for the animals - they're our midnight pals.

Becky Johnson (12)
Bettws High School

WHEN WILL SHE BE BACK?

As I sat in the car,
Angry and upset,
I thought,
Why had she gone?
When will she be back?

Was it that she didn't love us,
Or she didn't care,
Or that she'd just had enough
And was in despair?
I'm so depressed, angry and upset,
I just need to know . . .
When will she be back?

Ami Churcher (13)
Bettws High School

COME BACK MUM

Come back Mum.
Why did you leave?
Jan has to cook,
It makes me heave.

Come back Mum,
Dad's upset.
He forgets to pay the bills,
We're getting into debt.

Come back Mum,
I'm really scared.
You would come back,
If you cared.

Charlotte Jennings (13)
Bettws High School

COME HOME!

My mum has left me,
My boyfriend dumped me,
Nothing's going right,
Everything's going wrong.
Why is everything happening to me?
She's left with no trace,
No note, no call,
Just nothing.
I think my world is falling,
Falling away without a care,
Just like her.
I long to see her face again.

Lee-Ann Wellington (13)
Bettws High School

YOUR BAD DREAMS

I am your bad dream
I'm not as bad as I seem,
I may be a little scary
So be a little wary!

I am your bad dream
I may be a little mean
If you turn off your light at night,
I will give you an awful fright!

I am your bad dream
All dreams work in a team
I will come to haunt you
Look under your bed, boo!

Jamie Smith (12)
Bettws High School

SPORT

Cricket, tennis, swimming and football
Rugby, running and maybe netball,
Every sport, nearly every sport,
Is better than being in court.
Football is the best of all,
It says on my window and on my wall,
Football, rugby, then comes swimming,
Cricket, tennis, then the hard running.
Rugby is violent, serious and rough,
Even the skinny ones go in hard and tough,
Just sit back and watch the games
And listen for the important names.

Adam Blake (13)
Bettws High School

WHY SHOULD I?

My head is filled with confusion,
Emotions go wild in my heart.
Everything is changing now,
Why did Mum depart?
I'm mad at her but I love her,
She makes me feel helpless and sad,
Why did she leave Dad, Kev and me?
It couldn't have been that bad.
I don't want to take Mum's role,
After all, I am only sixteen,
But I can't go and leave like Mum did,
I couldn't be that mean.
Dad is in a state,
He misses you so much,
He stares into his cups of tea
And shudders at my touch.
Kevin doesn't understand,
He just wants you at home,
He misses you so badly,
We all feel so alone.
Why can't you just come home?
Keep things just the same,
I hate you but I love you,
Why should I take the blame?

Cathy Robins (13)
Bettws High School

WAITING

In a dark place
in a spooky, cold hut,
lived a lonely old man
with a long, black, scruffy beard.

No family, no friends,
just him waiting, waiting for his life to end,
surrounded by trees and huge, rocky mountains
which are flowing with water.

So silent,
So creepy,
Not a creature to be heard.

No food,
just dirty, polluted water,
always sitting in his hut
under a ragged, dusty, old book shelf,
sobbing, praying, waiting.

As he watches the sun go down,
he wonders what could be out there behind those cliffs,
hoping that one day, he'll wake up and discover
it was all a dream.

Waiting, waiting, waiting.

Danielle Bolt (11)
Bettws High School

SOMEONE ELSE

I feel as if I'm someone else,
My feelings are so mixed and muddled
But at the same time, I have no feelings,
Everything around me is different,
It's all changing, slowly but steadily.

How could she leave us
Alone, angry and annoyed?
I miss my mum, she's vanished
With someone she doesn't know.

I feel as if I'm warily alive,
I'm angry with her for leaving me
Her responsibility for being a mum for Kevin,
But I'm happy that she's not dead.

I have feelings flooding in and out of me,
Coming in me and then leaving twice as fast,
I'm confused,
The days just pass by
And don't seem to have any meaning.

People used to speak to me
But now they just pass by,
Even my best friends seem to be
Passers by and have no meaning.

Leanne Pitman (14)
Bettws High School

TOWN

People walking,
People working,
People talking,
People running,
People shopping,
People eating,
People stopping and
People shouting.

'Six bananas for a pound.'
'Six bananas for a pound.'

Macdonalds is the best,
Burgers, chips and all the rest,
Sweets, chocolates, crisps and ice-cream,
There's nothing more you can get.

Clothes shops,
Stationery shops,
Food shops,
Pharmacy shops,
There's so many, I forget.

Now it's time to go home
To catch the bus,
Or shall I phone for a lift, that would be easy,
Or shall I walk and not be lazy?

Vicky Howells (13)
Bettws High School

THE DAY I WAS CROWNED KING

On the day I was crowned king,
people cheered.

On the day I was crowned king,
the sun shone brightly.

On the day I was crowned king,
Manchester United beat Arsenal fifteen nil.

On the day I was crowned king,
lions roared.

On the day I was crowned king,
mice squeaked.

On the day I was crowned king,
telephone's rang.

On the day I was crowned king,
Elvis Presley was brought back to life.

On the day I was crowned king,
stars shone brightly.

On the day I was crowned king,
wages went up.

On the day I was crowned king,
Wales won the Rugby World Cup.

Michael Walton (12)
Bettws High School

IS HE THE ONE I LOVE?

Confused, I gazed above to find
The shadow was Pete,
The one I might love.
I felt a fool, confused and shocked,
I blushed.
He came back, still remembered me.
I'd ignored him for so long in
My own selfishness,
Just like my mum.
Why did he return,
To prove a point or to make a scene?
'Sorry,' I grinned,
Confused and muddled by his reply
That seemed to me as though I had lied
When he replied, 'I'm impressed.'
What did he mean? So I asked.
He leaned across, was he going to kiss
Or would he miss?
I guess he did, when he asked me for a drink,
Coffee, it's OK I guess.
The warmth of my body changed,
Was it the heat of us?
I had better not dare to touch his face,
Or lick my lips,
But time had passed.
I needed to return to life,
Was Pete my path, or just a dead end?

Jenna Travers (13)
Bettws High School

HAMSTERS

Hamsters are big and small,
Any how they might bite,
Many like to play about,
Some just like to lay around.
They like to have lots of fun,
Every day they are ready to run,
Russian, Syrian and Chinese breeds,
So always give them what they need.

Rebecca Jones
Bettws High School

I AM A VICTIM

I am like a target to other bullies,
I come from the mountains, not like this town.
I like eating soft rolls because they are as soft as me.
My friends are those who are nice to me,
My enemies are the bullies.
I am happy when everybody leaves me alone.

Daniel Baiton (12)
Bettws High School

TICK-TOCK

Tick-tock the hands go round the clock,
Bong-bing the pendulum starts to swing,
The clock starts to chime,
This clock can tell the time.
Cuckoo, it's quarter-past two,
Must dash, can't waste time like you.

Matthew Fife (13)
Bettws High School

MISSING MUM

Mummy, Mummy why did you leave?
I cry so much it's hard to breathe.
Every night I get a fright,
Nightmares, nightmares, they're wrecking my life.
I don't want my teddy,
I just want my mum,
Not my dad or my thumb.

Michelle Price (13)
Bettws High School

AN OCTOPOEM

The person is my English teacher, shouting at the class,
The season is winter, as dull and boring,
The colour is white, like the chalk on a blackboard,
The food is black burnt toast, yucky as can be,
The furniture is a broken desk chair,
The animal is an angry bull, charging straight at you,
The place is a classroom, where he makes us work hard.

Beth Savage (12)
Bettws High School

I AM A VICTIM

I am a frightened little lamb
I come from a valley not so far away.
I like to eat grass, because it's as soft as me.
My friends are scared, as scared as me.
My enemies are foxes trying to hunt me down.
I'm happy when I'm on my own
I'm sad when people torture me.

Kayleigh Cooper (12)
Bettws High School

THE VALLEY

Extravagant, unique mountains peer over the tranquil pool
filling the valley,
Their wise oldness looks after the trees and lake,
The trees canopy the serene lake, looking after its natural beauty,
The turquoise water mirrors the snow-capped mountains.
An elegant eagle swoops down from her nest in a nearby pine tree
And her prey is captured.
The dark shadow slowly devours the mountains, slowly
climbing down them.
The lake and trees dissolve in the blackness,
Night has fallen, taking this beauty with it till morn.

Samantha Lillygreen
Bettws High School

ABANDONED

As I'm abandoned
Badly ignored
Always lonely
Now afraid
Did try to eat
Only wanted to be alone
Night and day homesick
Did what I was told all the time.

Natalie Willis (11)
Bettws High School

SEASONS

Autumn time is with us now,
The autumn leaves of red and brown
Are fast falling to the ground.

The winter is coming,
No more light nights,
Go to bed early
And have pillow fights.

Watch out for Hallowe'en,
It could give you a fright!
The winter is coming,
So hold on tight.

The winter brings Christmas,
That is a delight,
All the presents on the floor,
Santa knocking at the door.

Spring is coming,
The farmers are busy sewing,
Soon the crops will be growing.

Then the summer comes along,
Our merry hearts are full of song.

Once again we have light nights,
No more time for pillow fights.

Sea and sunshine for us all,
Hooray,
We are coming to Porthcawl.

Laura Tuck
Bettws High School

ALONE IN MY BEDROOM!

Alone in my bedroom
I'm wondering why
Day turns to night.
Thinking about it
I don't understand.
Why does it happen?
Oh why, oh why?

Alone in my bedroom
I'm wondering why
Water is clear.
Oh why, oh why?
Thinking about it,
I don't understand.
Has it always been this way
On this beautiful land?

Alone in my bedroom
I'm wondering why
Blue is called blue
And white is called white.
Thinking about it,
I don't understand
Why words contain letters.
Oh why, oh why?

Alone in my bedroom
I'm wondering why
I'm writing this poem.
Oh why, oh why?
And then I remember,
It's helping me out,
To understand what this world's about.

Lucy Marsh (11)
Bettws High School

I STILL LOVE HER

Alone in the back seat
As the world rolled by,
I was thinking of my mum.
Why did she go? She had deserted us.
I was in my own world of confusion,
I still love her.

I feel shaky when I remember
What we used to do.
I miss her kiss at night,
The nagging of her voice.
I still love her.

Why did she go?
What did she think she was doing?
I feel like someone else, all alone and angry.
I still love her.

I'm all alone, what shall I do?
People stare at me all day through.
I'm tired, I'm angry,
I'm alone, I'm scared,
I'm all alone and nobody cares.

Why didn't she tell me?
Why didn't she say?
I hate her,
I love her,
I just want her here to stay.

Sara Millichip (14)
Bettws High School

SHOPPING

Saturday morning, here we go again,
Seem to have to go whether there's sun or rain.
The car journey up there is long and boring,
What a way to spend your Saturday morning.
I hate shopping!

The big wide doors welcome you in,
The tannoy and speakers bellowing,
Under starters orders off she goes,
Up and down those colourful rows.
I hate shopping!

She runs and runs straight past the buns
And even faster she flies past the pasta,
She gets the coffee
But misses the toffee.
I hate shopping!

Potatoes, tomatoes, she gets them all
At the speed she's going, it's a wonder she doesn't fall.
As she goes past, the jelly starts to quiver,
The ice turns into a flowing river.
I hate shopping!

I'm sure she could win the *best* shopper's cup,
It's nice to go home and put our feet up.
It's nice to sit down and watch the telly
Drinking chocolate milkshake and eating strawberry jelly.
I love shopping!

James Shinton (11)
Bettws High School

BAD DAY

It's 7 o'clock,
Time to get out of bed,
Little do I know
What's lying ahead

For my day at school,
Lots of work to do,
Running very late
And I've lost my shoe.

It's 8 o'clock
And I'm on my way,
It's started to rain,
I'm having a bad day.

Already I'm soaked
And I'm half-way there,
The wind just blew,
Now look at my hair.

I've finally arrived
At my form, just in time,
Sit down for ten minutes
Have time to unwind.

It's dinner time already,
Not long to go now,
Feet are aching badly,
I'll manage somehow.

I'm walking home
Out of the school gate,
A car has just splashed me,
That's just great.

Eleanor Venables (13)
Bettws High School

THE DAY I PLAYED FOR WALES

They've told many, many tales
About the day I played for Wales.
The crowd, the noise, the roar,
All waiting for me to score.

England, the oldest enemy,
Knew nothing about our secret weapon, me.
In the papers it said I was quick,
Elusive, clever and very slick.

The news was spread around Malpas, I was in,
'You deserve it,' said Mum with a grin.
'Play your game, play to win,
Use your skills, you'll have them in a spin.'

For more than an hour not a pass,
I wandered around and looked at the grass,
Then Jenkins with a wonderful punt,
Gave me the chance to put us in front.

I took the pass on the run,
The flying winger had just begun,
I easily ran past one, two and three,
Scoring the try seemed very easy.

Yes, there's many stories and tales
About the day I played for Wales.
In the interviews that followed, I said
Bang! . . . I fell out of bed.

Yes, it was all too good to be true,
I guess I always knew,
Yet who knows, maybe one day there will be tales
About the day I really did play for Wales.

Simon Harvey (11)
Bettws High School

THE MILLENNIUM

In the new millennium,
Will things be the same?
I often sit there wondering,
Again, again and again.

We hear about all sorts of things
That will happen in this year,
I wonder if they will come true
And if we have anything to fear?

They've built this big Millennium Dome,
It's quite a sight to see
And every time I look at it,
It looks like a spaceship to me.

Then there's this Millennium Bug,
That most computers fear,
It really could mess things up,
At least that's what we hear.

I've heard it could stop machines
That could harm people's health
And that planes could fall out of the sky
And there may be no food upon the shelf.

I hope these things don't happen
And when I go to bed that night,
I hope I will wake up in the morning
And everything will be all right.

But we'll still have a party,
About that there is no doubt,
We'll see the year 2000 in
And '99 go out.

Melissa Arlett (12)
Bettws High School

MUMS

I can never understand mums
One minute they're shouting and screaming,
Then they have an urge for cleaning,
They rush around like a busy bee,
Then sit down with their biscuits and tea,
I think they've all gone mental, and even lost their mind,
But even though she shouts and screams, I love my mum,
She's one of a kind.

Sîan Evans (12)
Bettws High School

MY PETS

I have a dog called Roly,
I also have a cat, because Roly was lonely,
'We need more pets' said Dad, 'it's too quiet.'
I told my sister and she ran riot.
'Can I have a horse, Dad, or maybe a camel?'
'Hang on kids, or I'll just get you a mammal.'
So in the end, we had a mouse,
But we lost it in the house.

Kirsty Wallis (12)
Bettws High School

ME!

In a house, old and cosy too,
I live and sleep and eat,
My brother shares that home with me,
My sister too, she's sweet!
My school, it's not so far away,
And new to me, it's true,
It's to a castle that I go,
For lessons every day.
My hair is brown,
My eyes the same,
I've freckles small and neat,
My piano fingers long and slim,
Lizzy is my name!

Elizabeth Church (11)
Cyfartha High School

ME!

I am a boy who likes his food,
Bolognese and Chinese,
Brussels sprouts and scones, dripping with jam.
I like them all.

I am a boy who likes science fiction,
Star Wars, Star Trek, Men In Black and Dr Who. Dr Who?
I like them all.

I am a boy who likes school,
History, technology, IT and English
But homework . . . Yuk!

Michael Thomas (11)
Cyfartha High School

MY HAMSTER

My hamster's life:
There's not much to it
Not much to it.
She presses her pink nose
To the door of her cage
And decides for the millionth time
That she can't
Get out.
My hamster's life:
There's not much to it
Not much to it.
It's about the most boring
Life in the world
If only she knew it
She sleeps and she drinks
And she eats.
This process
She repeats.
My hamster's life:
There's not much to it
Not much to it.
You'd think it would drive
Her bonkers
Going round on her wheel
It drives me bonkers
Watching her do it.
My hamster's life:
There's not much to it
Not much to it.

But she may be thinking
That my life
There's not much to it
Not much to
It at all.

Siân Burke (12)
Cyfartha High School

MYSELF

Bradley David is my name,
Practising Jujitsu is my
favourite game.
I've learnt to throw,
I've learnt to fall,
but it hasn't helped me,
to get up in the morning at all.
My favourite programme,
has a boy called Bart,
sometimes Mam thinks,
I should have the part!
I have two brothers,
Aaron and Scott.
Perfect like me they are not,
but they tell me I've lost the plot.
My room is always spick and span,

that's all because of the cleaner I call Mam.
I think I am perfect in every way.
I polish my halo every day.

Bradley David (12)
Cyfartha High School

THE RAGING SEA

Silent is the sea,
No waves can be seen.
I would love to go sailing,
I've always been keen.
One day I made a boat.
I decided to get away from it all.
I thought it would be fun,
I thought I would have a ball.
I had my own boat,
A boat all to myself.
'Gosh,' I thought,
This is the best day of my life.
But it didn't quite turn out like that,
The waves began to turn,
The wind began to pick up.
I was doomed to death, I learnt.
Then I could not believe my eyes,
A fancy cruiser came sailing by,
'Hop on board' the fat man said.
'Wow' I thought I was as good as dead.

Rhian Elin James (12)
Cyfartha High School

RUGBY

Rugby is such a wonderful game
It puts every other sport completely to shame.
It boasts a world full of famous players,
Jonah Lomu, Rob Howley, I don't know where to start.

The team I support is Merthyr Rugby Club
The clubhouse is nothing special, just an ordinary pub,
But Welsh rugby is definitely on the up.
At least now they've got a chance of winning the World Cup.

Wales have got great players,
Like Neil Jenkins and Craig Quinnell.
But my favourite's Alan Bateman who plays in the centre
You could say he is my rugby mentor.

But the greatest rugby men I will ever see,
Are my coaches at Merthyr, Alun and Shushee,
They teach us all there is to know,
Even if the game's off because of snow.

Thomas Few (13)
Cyfartha High School

ME, MYSELF

A winter baby, December 8th
Thea Meek was born
Mam and Dad were overjoyed
On that most joyful morn.

But joy turned to despair
When they got to know me
No sleeping, no eating
And no time for tea.

But as I've grown
They have come to see
The very best parts of me.

I think I'm very helpful
I think I can be kind
I'd like to believe that they think this
But really I don't mind.

Thea Meek (12)
Cyfartha High School

MY LIFE

Me and my family,
Not much to tell,
Parents apart,
But me and my sister are quite well.

We had two birds
My sister accidentally drowned,
Thought they could swim,
Also a cat that cannot be found.

Now I've got a dog,
That is bound to get knocked down,
You can't leave him alone,
Without him making a sound.

My friends and family,
All quite different,
In their own special ways,
But they are all magnificent.

My hobbies are sport,
Music and dance,
I can't go a day,
Without playing a prank.

Leanne Murphy (12)
Cyfartha High School

BEANO MAD

Some people say I'm Beano mad,
Some people think I'm childish.
Twice I've joined the Beano club,
Since I was quite youngish.

I could not give the Beano up,
Because it is so good.
I'd buy a double issue a week,
If I only could.

Nathan Wise (12)
Cyfartha High School

MY PARENTS

There are two people in my life,
They are called my mum and dad,
They ground me when I'm naughty
And comfort me when I'm sad.

They are the greatest people,
I really have to say,
I love them both dearly,
In every single way.

When I started nursery,
I was filled with fear,
But I wasn't nearly so scared,
When I knew my mother was near.

When the snow would start to fall,
I would go out to play,
My father would soon follow
And we would play all day.

They've always done their best for me,
This I have to say,
I hope with all my heart,
I'll repay them some day.

Siân Martin (12)
Cyfartha High School

AUTUMN

Autumn wears . . .
A coat of fiery woven leaves, russet, gold, scarlet and burgundy
edged in morning dewdrops.
Autumn moves . . .
Gracefully over the last traces of summer as the flowers
die away.

Autumn looks . . .
All dishevelled as the wind whips around her causing
her eyes to water with the chilly climate.

Autumn gives . . .
The world her one last glance as she walks away leading
winter by the hand.

Rebecca Moyles (11)
Cyfartha High School

LATE AT NIGHT!

A crash of thunder and flash of light
it always seems to happen at night
the rain hitting hard upon the window pane
hear my heart beat fast again.

A rumble, a roar, then a tap at the door.
I feel two arms around me tight
I hear a voice saying it'll be alright.

Slow and steady my eyes shut tight,
I didn't wake up until it was light,
No more rumbles, no more roars,
I have survived once more.

Natasha Jones (12)
Cyfartha High School

ME

My name is Emma and I'm really happy,
Except when I'm changing my brother's nappy.

My name is Emma and my dad's nearly forty,
Unlike me he's not very sporty.

My name is Emma and life can be funny,
Especially when I've got lots of money.

My name is Emma and I love the sun,
Playing outside is heaps of fun.

My name is Emma and homework's a bore,
It makes my hand extremely sore.

My name is Emma and I'm a wrestling freak,
I watch it nearly every week.

My name is Emma and I like to write,
I put my thoughts in my diary each night.

My name is Emma and I love playing cards,
But Mam always cheats and makes winning quite hard.

So it's Emma, Emma, you know my name,
If you haven't got it by now it's such a shame.

Emma Burke (11)
Cyfartha High School

IN THE MIRROR

When I look in the mirror,
I see a face,
With pinky skin and rosy cheeks.

When I look in the mirror
I see eyes,
Bright sparkling eyes.

When I look in the mirror,
I see lips as pink as pansies,
Sitting on the window sill.

When I look in the mirror
I see all these,
But is it really me?

When I look in the mirror
Do I see what's behind those sparkling eyes
And in my heart?

Do I see what I think of the world,
Or those who are in it?

I sometimes wonder,
What do I really see?
And is this really me
In the mirror?

Hannah Taylor-Kensell (12)
Cyfartha High School

MY SPORTING AMBITION

I enjoy sport of every kind,
It develops the body and broadens the mind.

The sport that most appeals to me,
Is our national sport, the game of rugby.

Rugby is a physical game,
And I'm proud to have such a famous name.

My ambition is to play for Wales,
Known in France as Pays des Galles.

For many years we have been in decline,
But now Graham Henry has made us shine.

In September I held the Rugby World Cup,
Let's all hope Rob Howley will next lift it up.

Jonathan Davies (11)
Cyfartha High School

THE BARK!

What is that barking noise?
Where are all the girls and boys?
Who is in Cyfartha Park?
What is making the dreaded bark?
Is it Crawshay haunting the castle?
Why is he giving us so much hassle?
The coldness of the ghosts and ghouls,
Spread around Cyfartha School,
Why is it suddenly going dark?
It's the curse of the howling bark!

Daniel Stickler (12)
Cyfartha High School

MY WEEK

Sunday . . . swimming,
Monday . . . swimming,
Tuesday . . . swimming,
Wednesday . . . cycling and running,
Thursday . . . swimming,
Friday . . . swimming,
Saturday . . . swimming,

Train, train, train.
Am I insane?

Saturday . . . competition,
nerve-racking, exciting,
frightening, thrilling,
exhilarating, nail-biting.
Sometimes delighting,
sometimes disappointing.

Lewis Bevan (12)
Cyfartha High School

SUN RAY, SUN RAY

Sun ray, sun ray sparkling bright,
where do you go to in the night?
Did you come from heaven above
Swirling down as a swooping dove.
Lighting everything so much.
Glistening, glowing with your touch?
Sun ray, sun ray sparkling bright,
Where do you go to in the night?

Adam Ridley (11)
Cyfartha High School

THE IMAGINATION

Many will describe him as a dark soul - a spirit that
feeds on death and carnage.
He is no man, woman, beast or child, but an immortal
cursed to walk the Earth since the dawn of time.
He walks the Earth endlessly, ending one generation and
beginning another.
He will squeeze the life out of you, as your soul emerges
he traps it.
Deep, deep in the heavens, each star holds one of his
precious whispering galleries.
In each gallery lie countless millions of souls, dying hopes,
dreams, sorrows and fears will shine and echo in
the vast endless reach of space for all eternity.

Kristian James (12)
Cyfartha High School

MY DOG SPROCKET

My dog Sprocket is a funny sort
He was found, he wasn't bought.
He had no collar had no name,
We often wonder from where he came.

His eyes are brown his nose is too,
A wagging tail to welcome you.
Four white paws, a furry face,
No other dog could take his place.

He's the best friend I've ever had
He's always there when I am sad
He'll look at me as if to say now
Cheer up and come and play . . .

Adam Jones (12)
Cyfartha High School

THE SNAIL

The snail, with its swirly shell,
eyes on stalks and slimy skin,
is an alien creature right here on Earth.
It moves without moving,
no limbs or wings to help it along on its long,
slow journey to the end of the garden
to get a bite of lettuce
may take a day, even two,
but it still keeps going,
not appearing to be moving,
but moving, nonetheless.
Leaving its slimy, horrible mess.
It slides past the flowers,
past the ants' nest and bees,
it hovers past the house, the grass and trees,
it glides past the shed, the trellis and holly,
and when it gets there,
it eats a blue pellet instead.

Adam Wordley (15)
Llantwit Major Comprehensive School

SUICIDE

I just can't go on like this anymore,
I really don't have anything to live for,
All I do is scream and shout,
I can't seem to find a way out.

The drugs are calling out to me,
These feelings just won't let me free,
I've learnt life's last lesson,
I'm in the pit of deep depression.

I met a man in a long, dark cape,
He made me realise I had to escape,
I ran away without a hope,
I realised, I just couldn't cope.

I started to plan my way out,
I then realised, what life was about,
Although these feelings drive me round the bend,
I now know, the answer is not the end.

Lindsay Kempley (15)
Llantwit Major Comprehensive School

THE LAST IS THE LADY

Outside my house, that's where *she* stands
Never moves just holds out her hands
They're long and thin, old and bony,
There she stands, frail and lonely.

Her family and friends have since long gone
No trace of her past and how it once shone
The last in her line through circumstances suspicious and shady
The last in her line, the last is the lady.

For years she has just stood there
Watching, unable to share
The changes she has seen
Industrial from green.

The people will stop under her umbrella green
Never take notice of the ageing queen
Because when it rains they'll stop but won't see
The ageless beauty of the old oak tree.

Jon Jeffreys (15)
Llantwit Major Comprehensive School

THE FIGHTING FALCON

Like a lightning bolt across the sky,
The F16 was soaring high,
Flashing, turning, twisting, diving,
The F16 roared across the sky,
Its blazing guns,
Its speeding missiles,
All combined on a bandit's tail,
Boom! Crash! Flame!
A bandit down in flames,
Flashing, turning, twisting, diving.
The F16 roared across the sky.

Blazing across the morning sky,
The F16 was soaring high.
Flashing, turning, twisting, diving.
The F16 roared across the sky,
Its dancer's grace,
Its mighty engine,
All combined in a lightning streak,
Intercept! Intercept! Intercept!
A bandit down in flames,
Flashing, turning, twisting, diving,
The F16 roared across the sky.

Streaking across the midday sky,
The F16 was soaring high,
Flashing, turning, twisting, diving,
The F16 roared across the sky,
Its flashing canopy,
Its dart-like body,
All combined to an unexpected grace,
Turn! Twist! Dodge!
A bandit down in flames,
Flashing, turning, twisting, diving,
The F16 roared across the sky.

Speeding across the night sky,
The F16 was coming down,
Slower, slower, careful, careful,
The F16 coming into land,
Its undercarriage down,
Its flaps ready,
The F16 gently touched down,
Slow! Slow! Stop!
The F16 down on the ground,
Careful, careful, careful now,
The F16 is home, at last.

Alex Branton (16)
Llantwit Major Comprehensive School

A BIRD'S EYE VIEW

Above the clouds, above the sky,
A lonely seagull soars on high,
Through tufts of candyfloss, wispy clouds,
And calls out into the darkness of night.

The sparkling stars look like diamonds so bright
And the moon gently shimmers on the great sea so white,
While the waves lap the shore with no care in the world,
The seagull flies into the darkness of night.

As dawn slowly rises, the shore becomes clear,
But no call from the seagull can anyone hear,
For below on the rocks lies a body so white,
That will never again see the darkness of night.

Lizzy Kelf (15)
Llantwit Major Comprehensive School

OF SOLIPSISTICAL CONTEMPLATION

A reflective edge on reality
To me seems to amass
Through the mortal's portals,
Far beyond the looking glass.

There is room, with a view on the soul
And for all that's trapped inside
To exercise a little potential,
While the truth has time to bide.

A revelation to the one,
A realisation that causes such shock?
With a Munch image of fear from
A considered stare to break the lock.

But everybody's high on traditional fallacy,
The present today is where existence thrives.
Yesterday's and tomorrow's memories are fallible
One of innate knowledge, nothing else survives.

And there is no desire for this life,
There's no tunnel with all the lights
Is there hope for another choice?
Upon a different plane set your sights.

Lucy Edwards (15)
Llantwit Major Comprehensive School

SANITY IS STATISTICAL

(Inspired by 1984, by George Orwell)

I loved then, I loved life
And showed intoxicating enthusiasm,
To any and all who crossed my well-planned path,
Inspiring them with my job at being alive.

It was not to last though,
My joy faded,
Replaced by exterior indifference,
Which poorly disguised the heavy burden of my knowledge.

I showed the signs of worry,
For the knowledge, I wish I had never acquired,
It ate away at my soul,
Stealing away from me, my socially acceptable self.

I despise who I had become,
A martyr,
Fighting for a cause,
Lost under the sheer numbers of my opposition,
Lost by the insanity of the principle,
Hoping that truth would prevail,
When society assured that truth safely contradicted itself,
For the good of all: not one.

'Sanity is not statistical,'
Well, perhaps if you have the strength, no stupidity, to believe,
When all around you,
Life is formed by the majority,
Rules are formed to the good of society
And individuality - a social taboo,
Ridiculed, dismissed as insanity.

Society is always right!

Julia Williams (15)
Llantwit Major Comprehensive School

THE STORM

The sky is pure and clear
Waves lapping softly on the shores
Sun shimmering in the sea
Birds singing in the warm air.

Far at sea, the sky is darkening
the waves strive for height
smashing mercilessly into each other
locked in an eternal fight.

The rain is fast and hard
pounding the sea endlessly
full of bitter hatred
for the great grey sea below.

The thunder bangs the sky above
smashing up the clouds
Lightning lights the horrific scene
showing the truth to all.

The storm thrashes on
no thought for those ahead
wrecking the tranquil scene
leaving only havoc in its wake.

Laura Whitby (15)
Llantwit Major Comprehensive School

THE BRAIN

The centre of a huge city,
With red roads and blue pavements,
Controlling the flow of red and white cars,
Millions of criss-cross wires connect the city network.

A huge memory bank in one corner of the city collects data,
A hi-tech defence system capable of killing all enemies,
A precise machine controls the network,
While a highly sensitive decoder collects information
about the surroundings.

Never mind Washington, London, Paris, Rome,
This is the capital of humanity.

Will Ambrose (16)
Llantwit Major Comprehensive School

WINTER

As winter closes in,
Ice, snow and wind will bring,
Darker nights, colder days,
Robins arriving, hedgehogs hide away.

As winter is well and truly here,
Christmas trees, lights and reindeer,
Bring smiles to faces all around,
Bells and carols, are the only sounds.

As winter draws to a close,
Blossoming trees, an early rose.
Snowmen melt and disappear,
Warmer days, spring is here!

James Page (16)
Llantwit Major Comprehensive School

FRIENDS

When times are good
And times are bad
You always need a friend.
They share your pain
And share your joy
And the friendship never ends.

Friends are there
Through thick and thin
And they're always by your side
They cheer you up
And make you smile
No matter how much you've cried.

Friends are one
Of the greatest gifts,
That anyone can get,
And if I were
To buy my friends,
They'd be the highest bet.

If I get ill
and have three hours to live,
and I want the world to end,
I hope the one thing
That's by my side
Is all of my dearest friends.

Samantha Roberts (15)
Llantwit Major Comprehensive School

THAT'S ALL I WANT

I want to have friends
I want to have fun
I want to be needed
By anyone.

I want good grades
I want a good life
I want a good job
And to be a good wife.

I want my own house
Not big, just small
I want my own car
An old one, that's all.

I want to be loved
I want to be cared for
I want to be happy
That's all I ask for.

I don't want a lot
As you can see
I just want the basics
Like anybody!

Kim Sewell (16)
Llantwit Major Comprehensive School

FLASH OF THE MIND

Screwed up
I need help
I'm hungry
Must have chocolate
More biscuits.

What are you doing?
Dunno
Don't ask me
I haven't got a clue
I want to go to bed.

That'll do
Leave me alone
I don't have to do anything
Why the hell are you asking me?
I haven't thought of anything.

Why are buildings called buildings?
Cos they're already built
I haven't got a clue
I need help
Screwed up.

Gemma Davies (15)
Llantwit Major Comprehensive School

GOD'S RICH ADORNING

The autumn sun gently gleams through the morning mist.
Dappled patterns from rugged oak trees, fall onto the earth below.
Dew encased cobwebs, glisten and flutter in the breeze,
Small and fragile, while the castle stands defiantly in the background.
The castle's ailing turrets suggest it was once majestically perched
upon the mound,
Standing bold on the horizon.
An enchanting glimpse of the past.
The mottled verdant ivy entwines itself amongst the gnarled and
withered rocks,
Charcoal-black with age,
Engulfed by lichens and dented with cracks where the ivy clings with
its pernicious fingers.
It squeezes the stones, forcing the castle to gasp for breath.
Nearby, the water bubbles and skips over pebbles in the brook,
so serene and calm.
The ferocious wind terrorises leaves on trees,
Whipping their midribs trying to pluck them from their mother branch.
Crows caw and navigate under the castle arches,
Squabbling sparrows chatter loquaciously, echoing throughout the ruins
and into the village below.
Morning has broken with God's rich adorning.

James Norman (15)
Llantwit Major Comprehensive School

THE SKY

One day people will fly
Fly so high, they'll touch the sky.

Clouds are fluffy
The air is stuffy.

Birds can fly non-stop
Until they reach planet pop.

The sky is so beautiful
With all its colours.

Birds will carry people on their back
Until they bring the whole world back.

The sky is cloudy now and then
When will it snow again?

The sun shines in the sky
The rain is from the clouds.

In the night the stars are out
Singing whatever they want.

Look at the man in the moon
He said he'll see you soon.

Zoe James (12)
Mynyddbach Comprehensive School

THE ELEPHANT

An elephant is a grey mouse standing on the trees.
An elephant is bigger than a house
Nose so big and so long,
So he cannot blow it.

He tramps around the grass
So the slimy snake falls off the trees,
Down on the grass with his tusks pointing south
Flapping back his ears, he stamps on the ground.

Round and round he goes
He will never die
He is the biggest you have ever seen
You will never forget him,
The big elephant.

Sarah Barry (12)
Mynyddbach Comprehensive School

THE SEA

The sea is my destiny
The sea is my life
The sea is my friend
The sea is yours
The sea is what you want to be
The sea has everything
The sea is full of fish
The sea is blue
The sea loves everyone
The sea is beautiful.

Sammy Lewis (12)
Mynyddbach Comprehensive School

A MIXTURE

Soldiers always stamp
Cars go up the ramp.
Dolphins always gurgle
People being burgled.
Snow is falling heavily
Don't forget the baby.
The cloud is always fluffy
Coats are always stuffy.
Sheep go ba, ba
Children go la, la.
Children wake up to see the sky
Mother's always cooking pie.
Birds can always fly
Always passing by.
The leaves are changing colour
Among the open pillow.
The spring is coming near
Always see some fear.
Fish go gobble, gobble,
Always tie your bobble.

Lisa Davies (12)
Mynyddbach Comprehensive School

THE SUN

The sun is a gold coin on a blanket,
The sun is a ball of red.
The sun is an orange football,
The sun is round like the moon.
The sun is bright.
The sun is like a slice of cheese.
The sun is gold and comes to Earth and shines on me.

Natalie Lloyd (12)
Mynyddbach Comprehensive School

MILLENNIUM

The millennium is drawing closer,
People are excited.
Planning parties, what to have
Drink, food and chocolate we've got.
1000 years have passed us
Will anyone stop and think of that?
What will the future hold for us?
I guess we'll have to wait and see.
They might stop testing on animals,
They might get rid of cars,
They might get rid of teachers,
That would be my dream.
But no one knows, no one can say
It's just a big mystery.

Ceri Williams (12)
Mynyddbach Comprehensive School

A WITCH

Whizzing and fizzing
The wicked witch flies on her big broomstick
Ever so high.

She frightens the children
And makes them cry
Ever so loud
That she hears it in a cloud.

Whizzing fizzing round and round
The shooting star hits the ground.

Sarah Collins (11)
Mynyddbach Comprehensive School

GRAFFITI

Yesterday - all my troubles seemed so far away
But now I have done a stupid thing.
I was caught graffitiing.
I was writing:
Katie Luz Robert
I did not know that the police were behind me.
Until Darrel called me and I turned around.
The police grabbed me and placed me in their car.
I was frightened,
I did not know what would happen to me.
I thought my dad would kill me
But he didn't because nothing would be solved.
I was grounded instead.
Tomorrow - I'll never do it again
Because I don't want to be grounded
I let my parents down.
I have no intention of doing that again.

Katie Williams (12)
Mynyddbach Comprehensive School

FEAR

There's a black blotch on the sink
I cannot say, I can only think.
It has many strings coming out
It's climbing up the water spout.

I wash away the horror and pain
Until I see it once again.
It was crawling up on the pipe
It opened its eyes and saw the sight of its life.

Lisa Jones (12)
Mynyddbach Comprehensive School

THE SUN

The sun is a cheese cracker
The sun is a circle of fire
The sun is a globe of cheese
The sun is a bright light bulb
The sun is a big tennis ball
The sun is a smiley face
The sun is always yellow and bright
And the sun is my friend
The sun is a woollen yellow ball
The sun is a gigantic balloon
The sun is a lump of gold
The sun is glittery and shiny
So that's why I love my shiny sun.

Carly Thomas (12)
Mynyddbach Comprehensive School

LOOKING OUT OF THE WINDOW

The trees are rustling
The howling wind rushes by
The autumn leaves are falling day by day.
The birds are flying with glorious songs
Into the future the birds might not sing.
The trees might not come to autumn.
The houses will change.
The graveyards are silent.
The trees will die down
Until everything is silent.

Sarah Taylor (12)
Mynyddbach Comprehensive School

MY BABY COUSIN RUBY

A cute moaner
A milk drinker
A messy eater
A tearful cryer
A loud screamer
A happy soul
A toy lover
A Cuddly bear.

Amanda Palmer (15)
Mynyddbach Comprehensive School

THE SUN IS . . .

The sun is an orange football.
The sun is round as the moon.
The sun is bright.
The sun is a gold coin.
The sun is my reflection.
The sun is a golf ball.
The sun is like a piece of cheese.

Claire Evans (12)
Mynyddbach Comprehensive School

MY BROTHER

A lazy swine
A troublemaker
An attention seeker
A mad maniac
But he's my brother!

Helen Corbett (15)
Mynyddbach Comprehensive School

THE DRAGON

His sharp eyes follow you
His sharp claws scrape the floor
A red fire-breathing statue.
The protector of Wales.
His spiky tail is sprawled along
His cave of sleep.
No one dare enter
Not even a knight in shining armour.
For he will be no match
For this breathtaking sight.
His voice echoes through the
valleys afraid.
He will turn your blood blue
and freeze it too.
With his looks of horror
and burning breath.
He will make you yell and shout
for help!

Nerys Thomas (13)
Pen-Y-Dre High School

SNOW

The mountains are covered in a
blanket of white.
The children ride down on sledges.
The world seems to be covered in snow.
This frosty landscape - so cold and harsh.
A world cast in ice of magical appearance.
This cold but beautiful landscape.

Kelly Hamer (14)
Pen-Y-Dre High School

FOUR SEASONS IN ONE DAY

I'm in my bed one sunny morning,
I can't go to sleep
but yet I'm yawning.
I put my head under the pillow
I hear the cows start to bellow.

All of a sudden it starts to go dark
I look out of my window
there's no one in the park.
Then all of a sudden it starts to rain.
Please God make it sunny again.

I'm very cold and I'm shaking
as I walk - my back is aching.
I go downstairs to watch some telly,
then I heard a rumble in my belly.

It starts to rain
I put on my wellies,
I walk out of the door
with a pocketful of lollies.

I go down the hill on a sleigh
it starts to go dark . . .
I think it's the end of the day!

Michael James (13)
Pen-Y-Dre High School

SIMILES POEM

As handsome as a prince,
As clever as a mince,
As clean as a bean,
As weak as a leak.

As ugly as a bin,
As clean as a sin,
As mean as a bin,
As keen as a lim.

Sam Shipman (13)
Pen-Y-Dre High School

NIGHT-TIME

Time to climb the never ending stairs,
time to enter the cold, dark room
at the end of the winding passage,
time to climb into the cold
bed waiting for me.
Time to go to sleep . . .
I can't sleep, for every time I close
my eyes I see a snarling predator,
with huge eyes like dinner plates
And razor sharp fangs glistening in the dark
And a cruel snarl which makes
me as cold as ice.
Its huge shadow projected onto the wall,
I fear going to sleep in case it does come for me,
A continuous patting of rain on
my window makes me want to scream
and my continuos fear of the ravenous
beast also makes me want to scream.
I'm uncomfortable but don't make any stirring,
The beast is also uncomfortable
constantly stirring,
I don't move a muscle because I
know this huge, ravenous blood
thirsty predator is waiting . . . just waiting.

Linzy Phillips (12)
Pen-Y-Dre High School

WELSH RUGBY

14 months ago
Defeat after defeat after defeat
Then along comes a man
From New Zealand he was.
His name - Graham Henry,
The saviour, the redeemer.

He pulled the Welsh from the brink of peril.
Then he imported some players
From all over the globe
To play the world champs
And take them down to the wire.
He shocked the world,
All the women and men
And all the Welsh people
Had faith again!

The 5 Nations came
To Murrayfield we went.
But home we came
With a frown on our face.
Back to Wembley
It was a 2 horse race.
But again we lost
Because of that place.

Stade de France,
Here we come!
Henry's men are ready again.
The last minute came
We were up by a point
The final kick - a penalty
Up stepped Thomas.
Would it go over?
No it would not!

Wales broke the 24-year lock
With a win in Paris
It took long enough too!

To Wembley we went
With the English in mind.
Again it went down to the wire.
A line-out . . . in their 22
Then through went Gibbs,
And over he went.
But still one behind.
The conversion was vital
And over it went.
The Welsh had done it again.
32 - 31.

The World Cup is here
It's in our sights.
But we started it
With a couple of fights.
Suspended was Charvis
It just wasn't fair!
But we still scraped through . . .
So rumble on the Welsh!

David Kelly (13)
Pen-Y-Dre High School

THE LITTLE PIGLET

We walked up to the farmyard
And heard a chorus of grunts
On looking in the pigsty
We found a litter with a runt.

The sow was being motherly
Lying on her side
And all the little piglets
Were milking the poor sow dry.

But the smallest of the litter
Just sat and cried *Oink! Oink!*
As if to let his mother know
That he has had no milk.

When all his brothers and sisters
Had finished their evening meal
The little runt snook up to her
And tried to get his fair deal.

But after a few minutes
The weary sow ran dry
And so the little piglet
Let out a moanful cry.

The farmer came a running
To see what was the fuss
And he found the smallest piglet
Crying as if he'd been trussed.

The farmer's wife came viewing
And saw this little pig
His eyes were oh so sorrowful
And wished that he was big.

She picked him up and cuddled him
And took him to the house
Where she warmed a bottle of milk
To see if he wanted a drink.

Now that little piglet
Is a great big boar
The farmer takes him walking
For truffles on the floor.

Natalie Davies (14)
Pen-Y-Dre High School

NIGHT-TIME

It's time to climb the endless stairs,
I dread this part every night, the stairs,
are cold, dark and eerie and sends a
shiver up my spine.
Time to enter my cold, dark bedroom.
Time to climb into bed and this is the
worst part and try to go to sleep with
no light on!
I lie there for hours on end listening,
to the everlasting tick of the clock, then
there's the continuous movement of the big
hairy, ferocious beast under my bed
waiting for me.
There it goes again, the huge, lurking
shadow can be seen continuously moving
and waiting for me outside my closed
bedroom door.
The continuous roaring of car engines zooming past.
My eyes are slowly closing and I'm
Feeling sleepy . . . zzzzzz.

Leearna Lyons (12)
Pen-Y-Dre High School

WONDERFUL WALES

Music, pop, choirs and all
Catatonia, Stereophonics and Tom Jones stand so tall.
Performing to crowds in a whirl
Come on Kelly! Give us a twirl!
Male voice choirs over the valleys
Singing out their vocal qualities.
Charlotte Church a new sensation
On TV - her first presentation.

Mining - the industry never forgotten
Valleys - men would get so rotten.
Under the ground the boys would go
Instead of schooling with chalk and slate
They would get in such a state.

Castles used for the crossfire fights
Cardiff, Caerphilly, Carmarthen and all
Castles which were certainly not in mall.
Ruins now in no shape
For use is unreal
And they make you feel
Spooked and uneasy,
Perhaps a little queasy!

Mountains steep and very deep
Looking up they seem to reep.
Hanging on the sheep, they eat
The grass they eat they see as their feast.
Mountain walkers brave and rough
The task ahead seems too tough.
At the top they've had enough.

Welsh food unique in taste
Leeks and laver bread
Posh people eat instead
Welsh rarebit is great to eat
It's a shame the rabbit is the meat!

Rugby, Wales' favourite game.
The Welsh team are staring into fame.
Jenkins the ginger superman
Always there to give a kick.
He's always there to give a boost
Like a cockerel in the roost!

Lisa Hennessy (13)
Pen-Y-Dre High School

WALES

Stereophonics
And the Welsh flag,
Singing songs
About shopping bags.

Rugby World Cup
And silver spoons.
Wales are winning,
Because rugby rules.

Daffodils, leaks
And new-born sheep.
Chewing grass
From valleys so deep.

Up the hills
And down the mines,
Where people worked,
Making railway lines.

Millennium Stadium,
Was made in time.
It's been played in and won in,
We're ready to shine!

Rhiannon Meade (14)
Pen-Y-Dre High School

STUFFERATION

It comes from a freezer,
and everyone scoops it up,
Ice cream.
I like that stuff.

It melts away,
In no time at all,
Chocolate.
I like that stuff.

It carries CDs
And makes a lot of noise,
Music.
I like that stuff.

It's cuddly and small
And barks all day,
Dogs.
I like that creature.

It buzzes around
And sometimes stings,
Bees.
I hate that animal.

They get on your nerves
And can't stop laughing,
Boys.
I hate them.

They crawl on the floor
And makes a sss sound,
Snakes.
I hate them.

They run with the ball
And make a run,
Rugby.
I hate that game.

Marie Launchbury (11)
Pen-Y-Dre High School

SUN SMILES

The sun smiles down on the world
and happy is the word.
The sky is clear not a cloud in sight
everybody is feeling alright.

Buildings seem to smile,
they're happy in the sun.
Animals gazing peacefully
the day has just begun.

The sea is calm, it seems so still
it's glistening like gold.
It makes you want to hold.

The mountains are tall
and peaceful.
Their green, green grass
glitters like glass.

The birds are out and singing
they make you feel alive and kicking.

Then night falls, the sun
slowly hides.
We hope tomorrow's sun
comes up with the tide.

Taryn Smale (13)
Pen-Y-Dre High School

BLOOD ON THE TOWER

The wedding was set, in a church, in Paris
The background was beautiful, a day of sunshine.
The bride was dressed, groomed and plumed,
The groom was immaculate, tired and drunk.
The groom, as he tried to stand up, watched and waited,
As the bride, in brilliant white, glided down the aisle.
The guests watched and wailed as the good vicar
Married the couple with the Eiffel Tower in the distance.
The reception came and people were laughing,
The food was lovely, the wine even better.
And the groom was wooden all the way through,
As the time for speeches had come.
The best man stood up and thanked the people,
Thanked the cook and thanked the vicar.
The father stood up and did the same, then,
The time had come for the groom to speak.
He thanked everyone he could think of
Then he called for quiet, as he grew solemn.
'I would also like to thank Kevin the best man
And my wife, Bernadette, for having an affair.
And I hope they will be happy.'
With that, he ran to the tall tower
Climbed up and jumped into the river below.
Leaving Kevin and Bernadette gob smacked.

The reception ended up as a battleground,
With Kevin and Bernadette in the middle,
As bloodstained guests tiptoed over dead bodies
To try and get home.
And the families refused to go to the next wedding,
The wedding of Kevin and Bernadette.

Kelly Jones (16)
Pen-Y-Dre High School

RAINY DAYS

The rain is like an ocean,
like the waves going mad in a storm.
It makes us feel sad because
everything is gloomy.
The rain makes us feel like we don't
want to get up in the mornings
because everything is wet and dark.
We all wish that the sky would open
and the sun would come beaming down
but I don't think that will happen!
The rain is life-taking,
you never see anyone out.
It's boring!
Then summer is here again . . .
Everyone is out and the heat is beating down
on bare skin
and there is a stretch of blue sky above.
Everyone is happy again . . .
For summer's here!

Kylie Rees (13)
Pen-Y-Dre High School

NIGHT-TIME

The rushing traffic screeches as it comes to a
sudden halt outside,
The continuos dripping of taps on the dull,
metal sink makes you tremble.
That dark mysterious, ghostly figure on
the door turns out to be an old dressing gown.
That strange, squeaky voice of my sisters
sleep talking woke me up suddenly.
The dark, stone cold, never-ending stairs
Leads you to a dark and spooky room,
Floorboards creak loudly as you nervously walk
up to your room.
The yellow fanged monster in your dream
wakes you up with a sudden scream,
What's that terrible, crucifying noise under
your bed, maybe a monster.
The pair of trousers that hang out through
the slightly open door looks like a man,
there's a ghostly white figure in the darkest
corner of the room,
as you awake you realise the tick ticking
of the clock is not very spooky at all.

Danielle Clark (12)
Pen-Y-Dre High School

THE CLASH OF THE TITANS

Thrust into darkness
The sky has turned black
The Titans are coming
They're ready to attack

A thunderous roar
A spear of light
Sent by the Gods, into the night

A tingle in the air
Sends shivers down my spine
The wind is getting stronger
It's only a matter of time

The heavens have opened
Down pours the rain
Battering against the windows
Running down the drain.

Helen Jones (13)
Pen-Y-Dre High School

FEAR IS . . .

Fear is a dark alley with its glowing, ghostly street lamps
and a never-ending wall of shadows that are lurking helplessly
over you like a creeping cloud of smoke.
Fear is a long, open land with the distinctive sounds of owls
waking, with an unexpected airy breeze which gives you tingles
to the upper spine.
Fear is a graveyard where many people lay alone in the lowered coffins.
The stone of memory gives off an evil sheen.
Fear is being abandoned near an historic castle where you look up and
see the tower's open and winds cast moving shadows on your face.
Fear is a dark closed-off room with shut-off windows and black, damp
walls with cobwebs and you can barely see in the corner. As I follow up
the broken paint I see a picture of what looks like a devil.
Fear is not knowing what happens next, who you see and what they do.
You get frustrated and fall violently on the hard floor and cover your
tearful face so as not to see what's going on.
You give off an annoying scream.
You've got no energy
You can only
Suffer!

Amy Thomas (14)
Pen-Y-Dre High School

FEAR

Fear the slimy slithery snake or any mouse or
edible animal, he will devour in a gulp.

The snake slithered slightly closer to its prey
in a side winding movement.

The sly snake slithers to a halt, his unsuspecting
prey now in his sight.

The creepy crawly slithery snake cunningly waits
and waits to pounce.

His darting dastardly tongue touching the scent of
his prey in the air.

His mouth stretches boiling hot gleaming deadly fangs
as he pounces and poisons his prey.

The screaming of the rats chest crushing as the
snake closes its jaw and devours it.

The slithering sliding snake disappears into hiding
once more ready to pounce again on his next
unsuspecting prey.

Adam Pollard (13)
Pen-Y-Dre High School

PEOPLE

People come in all shapes and sizes,
Fat, thin, round, short and tall.
People have all different kinds of names,
Gina, Jackie, Robert and Paul.

Some people are black and some people are white,
And some are a bit in-between,
Some people are poor and some people are rich,
You can't help what's in your genes.

People have all different kinds of religions
That they worship night and day.
All different people have all different birthdays,
June, September, January and May.

To me it doesn't matter, the shape, the race or size,
All that really matters is the content of the character,
What is on the inside is all that really applies.

Lauren Bellshaw (13)
Pen-Y-Dre High School

GAVIN EVANS - MY KIND OF GUY

My person should live on top of a mountain
So the rest of the world can see him.

He is kind and soft like water
He is clean and green like water.

He is soft, friendly and furry like a cat
Which sat on a soft mat.

His voice sounds soft and clear
Like a violin.

He looks like a sunny summer's day
When it's raining.

Pop music is his style
He is lively - like the songs.

His saying is 'I don't believe it!'
When things go wrong.

Gavin Evans (15)
Pen-Y-Dre High School

CRUST OF WHITE

Snow, snow, it lays across the land,
wherever you look.
The cold chilling carpet that blankets
the land in a crust of white.
And then there's a beautiful side.
The cool air, where fun's only around the corner.
It clings to rooftops and chimney pots.
Like a cat it creeps into every crevice.
As if, as if it's been there since eternity.
The flakes, gliding through the sun's rays,
melting each little flake one by one.
The sun's rays - could they have arrived?
No, a minor break in the clouds and then
the snow breaks through again.
The deathly silent hilltops.
As silent and as still as a tree with no wind.
Streets deserted. Cars abandoned.
Suddenly it's cold, too cold and fun's
no longer around the corner.
The cold chilling carpet that blankets
the land in a crust of white.

Craig Beard (13)
Pen-Y-Dre High School

IF I COULD CHANGE THE WORLD

If I could change the world,
I'd make cars fly on air,
I'd recreate men and women
And create them with wings instead.

I'd change the schools and teachers,
Banish them one by one,
I'd fill their bags with crawly creatures
Then watch them scream and run.

Everyone would travel on elephants,
Giraffes and camels too,
I'd make the cows go quack
And make the ducks go moo.

But then it's still a dream
Of owning gold and pearls,
Me and my friends would live like queens,
If I could change the world.

Natalie Jones (13)
Pen-Y-Dre High School

FRIENDSHIP

Our friendship is very special,
Which you and I should see,
The reason it's so special
Is it's just for you and me.

If ever we are lonely
Or feeling down and blue,
We only have to read this poem
And we'll know it's always true.

Friends are always there when needed,
Sticking by like glue,
Through the good days and the bad days,
They are always there for you.

You never can break it,
It's always there for good,
We will stay friends for ever,
Just like best friends should.

Sarah Farr (13)
Pen-Y-Dre High School

IN MY HOUSE . . .

In my house and up the stairs,
My mother's plucking out plughole hairs.

My father's looking for his driving book,
Shouting to everyone to 'get and look.'

My sister Zoe, she's such a freak
Acting as if she's a little sheep.

I have three more (sisters I mean)
Two of them playing dancing queens.

My sister Lucy, youngest of all,
Crawling everywhere, crawl, crawl, crawl.

James, Jacob, my two other brothers
Running around nagging my mother.

These are the people in my house,
At night quiet, quiet as a mouse.

Rhiannon Evans (14)
Pen-Y-Dre High School

SEASONS

Spring is when the world wakes up
a time to sing and dance
Chicks and lambs are being born
and chocolate eggs are given.

Summer is when the sun comes out
and people go on holidays
Ice-cream dripping on the floor
and loads of ransacked beaches.

Autumn is when the leaves start falling
yellow, orange, red and brown
Harvest brings in all the corn
and animals set in for hibernation.

Winter is when the nights get shorter
snow may fall and decorations go up for Christmas
Little stockings at the end of the bed
waiting for Santa to fill them.

Kate Morgan (12)
Pen-Y-Dre High School

DRIVING ALONG

I am in a car driving along,
going really fast
from the past.
Rain hitting the windscreen
making me scream,
wheels start spinning
car starts turning.

Ahead of me I see
a ship in the sea
I'm wondering what's ahead
will I end up dead?

A huge wall looms up
so I want to erupt
but I try to break through
the big tough wall,
but I don't succeed at all.

Adam Williams (15)
Pen-Y-Dre High School

AUZZIE

I was living in Australia
In a Eucalyptus tree,
When suddenly I saw
This strange creature approaching me.

With wooden hockey stick legs,
In the shape of a V,
They were very funny I must agree.

With a mobile phone body
And an antennae as a neck,
With orange on the screen
And a circle around its neck.

I asked him what his name was
He said, 'My name is Auzzie,'
I asked him where he got it from
He said, 'From my body.'

He had a smell of flowers
And his voice sounded of rain,
He said he likes to paint,
He said, 'That's my Auzzie name.'

Lynsey Murphy (13)
Pen-Y-Dre High School

GANGLAND

The damp, murky streets
Where no one dare go once the sun sets
Are set alight by the crime and violence.

Every street is owned by gangs,
The children with their knives
And the elderly man with his shotgun
Protecting his disabled wife.

The screams in the night fade into a vacuum
The gunshot heard but nobody listens
The screech of car tyres, the cry of a mother.

Morning has broken, new light, new hope,
A mother sends the boy to school,
Trying to save him from the grasp of the gangland.

Matthew Davies (17)
Pen-Y-Dre High School

FEAR IS . . .

Fear is walking into the smoky darkness,
You don't know if something spooky is there,
Blood curling up your spine.

Fear is bristles and a flash of fangs
You feel skeleton legs of a spider
Eyes peering from the foggy mist
You run through with fear.

Fear is walking past a graveyard
Where there are no lights on
A ghost is sitting up
And you are running down.

Fear is walking through a black hole
Don't know where to go
You're walking into a ghost train
With skeletons hanging down.

Fear is running through a spooky place
You're trying to keep to the pace
You've just been in a race
You won the very big chase.

Paula Hughes (13)
Pen-Y-Dre High School

I Wish . . .

I wish
I wish that I was famous
I wish
I wish that I could win the lottery
I wish
I wish that I could be a queen
I wish
I wish that I ruled the world
I wish
I wish that I could go wherever I wanted
I wish
I wish that I lived in a mansion
I wish
I wish that I could have any animal that I wanted
I wish
I wish that I could have any sports car that I wanted.
I wish . . . I wish!

Cerys Cook (12)
Pen-Y-Dre High School

Similes Poem

I'm as handsome as a newborn boy
As a brand new toy
As a puppy that has been born
As a piece of paper that has not been torn.

I'm as clever as a devil in hell
As a child listening for a bell
As a clever box
As a fox.

I'm as clean as a glass of water
As the queen's son and daughter
As a baby pig
As my granny's wig.

I'm as strong as Sporty Spice
As a pong after curry and rice
As a piece of fudge
As Mr Tudge.

Natalie Etheridge (12)
Pen-Y-Dre High School

MY LITTLE GREEN ALIEN

My little green alien lives in a town
Where they sit on the ceiling and eat
Upside down.
They drink through their noses and
Talk through their ears.
My little green alien how weird he is.

My little green alien burps through
His bum
He mates in a tree and lives with
His mum.
His head is funny, his arms are his legs
When they have babies they come out of eggs.

My little green alien has a few friends
And all of their roads have got lots of bends.
He drives a car that's back to front
The stupid green alien slipped in the mud.

Daniel Beattie (13)
Pen-Y-Dre High School

FEAR

Fear is a giant snake
Sliding over your feet
He can pounce at any moment
To him you're just meat.

Fear is my cousin Jared
Doing psycho wrestling moves
Using me as a punch bag
Kicking me with his size 12 shoes.

Fear, is a poltergeist
Smashing through a TV screen.
He's big, he's deformed and ugly
And he's not half-mean.

Fear is having cancer
Never knowing when
You've been told soon you'll be dead
It happens to women more than men.

Fear is being lost in a city
Looking with a sad helpless face
There she is, you've seen your mother
You don't half pick up the pace.

Adam James (13)
Pen-Y-Dre High School

STORM

The darkening blackened sky
The waving battered trees
The birds swooping through the
skies to seek shelter
The mountains are being washed away
With the flood of rain.

When morning comes
The river is swollen
and the fish have got an expanded home.
But the people who live on the river banks
are flooded with worries . . . not just water!

Lyndsey Rogers (13)
Pen-Y-Dre High School

RUNAWAY HILL

I am a passenger in a car,
We're driving on a motorway.
There is a woman driving
The traffic is terrible.
It's a cold, cloudy wet day and very busy.
Muddy hills, factories, lorries delivering goods.
There is a bridge ahead,
River clear and clean.

I see ahead of me a calm, peaceful place.
Children running and shouting.
No more factories to be seen
Just fields of green.

Blocking my way to this
beautiful place is a runaway hill.
A rusty iron door stands at the top.

The journey through I do not know.
My childhood I would like to see.
A knock or two upon this door
would bring the door open
for me.

Elizabeth Johnson (14)
Pen-Y-Dre High School

FEAR IS . . .

Fear is the icy cold fingers touching you in the dark.
Fear is the feeling of people watching you walking down a
deserted path.
Fear is going down the cellar and feeling a spooky atmosphere
around you.
Fear is . . . fear is . . . fear is . . .
Fear is hearing creaking and cranking on the floorboards in the night.
Fear is hearing footsteps coming up the stairs and across the landing in
the night.
Fear is the thought of hot burning eyes glaring through you.
Fear is . . . fear is . . . fear is . . .

Fear is seeing a flash of shiny fangs and blood dripping off them.
Fear is walking through the cemetery in the middle of the night and
hearing branches snapping somewhere else.
Fear is the noises behind you when you are far from home in the night.
Fear is . . . fear is . . . fear is . . .

Shane Small (13)
Pen-Y-Dre High School

A CHRISTMAS RHYME

Christmas comes but once a year
On the 25th it will be here,
Lots of presents under the tree
Especially for my brother and me.

I wake up in the morning
Wishing it would snow,
So I could go out playing,
Till my hands and feet are cold.

I'd go out carol singing
Hoping to get a penny
And wish them a Merry Christmas
If they didn't give me any.

A couple of days later
It will be the millennium
I'll never see another
So I can't wait for 2001.

Rhydian Patterson (12)
Pen-Y-Dre High School

WINTER

October is cold
Leaves are falling off the trees
Time for fancy dress.

November is wet
It lights up the sky at night
Guy Fawkes is burning.

December is fun
Santa comes with your presents
Hang up your stockings.

January it snows
It's time for new resolutions
It's a new year.

February love
It is time for Valentines
It is a leap year.

Cheryl Evans (11)
Pen-Y-Dre High School

A PLAGUE OF FLAKES

Like tiny feathers
They blow with the wind
Each with their own shape
So soft, so delicate.

They cover the earth's surface
Like sugar icing on a cake
Where do they come from?
Are they more than just flakes?

The town is so quiet
No one's around
Animals are hid
Making no sound.

It's a plague of flakes
That are so cold
But I don't mind
My story's told.

Taryn Rachel Evans (14)
Pen-Y-Dre High School

PANDA

P retty panda black and white, in the jungle of the night
A nd even when you're sleeping, the world outside is peeping.
N ear or far, no matter where you are, I know you are still true.
D rawn as a picture printed on paper, black and white, you
    are and you will always be.
A nd if you have a baby I hope it all goes well, I might never
    see you again so I guess this means farewell.

Stacey Price (11)
Pen-Y-Dre High School

MY DREAM

Present:
I was travelling across the sea
in my speed boat
and the weather was cold and wet.
I was thinking how am I getting to my future
when I was thinking
I reached a great wave
that I needed to get past
so I put my foot down and got over the wave.

Future:
As I got past the wave
I got to my island Ibaze
with an extraordinary big house
palm trees all round the house
with the baking hot sun around.

Craig Baylis (14)
Pen-Y-Dre High School

SUNNY DAYS

The sun is shining down on us,
We're glowing so bright like gold.
The sun is one thing which we
all would love to hold.
In our arms each day while wishing
for our problems to fade away.
Into that sun shining so bright
that clears that sky - day and night.

Leanne Mew (13)
Pen-Y-Dre High School

FEAR

Fear is the spine chilling howls from a
mysterious creature lurking in the eerie forest.
Fear is the gruesome monster hiding
under your childhood bed.
Fear is the silent screams of lost souls in
an unnerving cemetery.
Fear is creeping spiders that make your
skin crawl and your hair stand on end.
Fear is the icy stare from a beast as it
hides in the shadows.
Fear is an unearthly being gazing
satanicly at you through the darkness.
Fear is the demons that torment you
through the long dark night.
Fear is death hanging anxiously over
you until the day you die.

Lee Bowditch (13)
Pen-Y-Dre High School

AS LONG AS WE BEAT THE ENGLISH!

Come on Wales sing it,
Got beaten by the Irish,
Got beaten by the Scots,
The French had a strudel,
But as long as we beat the English,
But as long as we beat the English we don't care.
We don't care!
So come on England we know you are crap!

Jamie Lucas (11)
Pen-Y-Dre High School

SCHOOL

The bell goes, it's half-past eight,
everyone goes to registration.
The bell rings again, it's lesson one,
the corridors packed, we all get squashed.
We get to our lesson all tired and puffed out.

The loud teachers screech 'Sit in your chair.'
We're all working hard waiting for the bell,
then it's lessons two, three and finally four.
The bell goes for dinner, everyone runs,
they are like a herd of elephants,
it is like feeding time at the zoo.

Then it's lessons five and six,
the bell goes for the end of school.
All the children pour out of every door,
they run like lava running from an erupting volcano.

Rebecca Jones (13)
Pen-Y-Dre High School

FEAR

The evil-eyed monster was staring at me from the hallway,
The slither of a slimy snake, as it slithers along the hot deserted path,
The long see-through ghost was staring at my nan in a photo,
The fearsome fangs and the devil-like eyes peering in the hallway,
The bony white skeleton walked across my landing
shaking its bony bones.
The sound of eerie footsteps walking up the stairs,
The evil-eyed snake was shaking its rattling tail in the hot desert.

Lauran Brown (13)
Pen-Y-Dre High School

NIGHT-TIME

The crackling noise of the wooden floorboards creaking is
lingering on and on.
And the irritating tingling of the clock ticks fast in the silence of
your room.
The shadows are creeping quietly up onto your bedroom wall as
you tensely watch.
Then the roll of thunder and the flash of lightning sends a shiver
down your spine as you are sitting up nervously in bed.
The wind is howling and whistling as it sways the trees back and forth
as they bash against your window.
The thought of a monster creeping quietly up onto your bed is getting
very tense.
The mighty rain is lashing against the window like symbols banging
together.
And then all goes quiet and you grab the chance to get to sleep.

Hayley Jones (12)
Pen-Y-Dre High School

FEAR

Fear is a wolf howling its heart out
In the middle of the gloomy forest,
Fear is a flash of red eyes peering
Though a deserted cottage,
Fear is a cave, full of blood
Thirsty cats
Fear is a sudden flash coming from
A deserted lighthouse.

Christian Lewis (13)
Pen-Y-Dre High School

THE FRILLY DRESSED CLOWN

I was on my way to school
At 7.30 in the morning.
I saw an ugly creature moaning,
She had a pink frilly dress on
And a head like a clown,
She also wore a great big frown
I asked her what was wrong.
She sang me a horrid song,
It was called boom, boom, boom.
I asked her where she lived,
She said a Sulo bin.
I replied that's why you stink.
We said goodbye
She started to cry
And I walked off to school.

Katie Barrett (12)
Pen-Y-Dre High School

FEAR

The eerie sounds of a piercing scream from a helpless young
Woman, echoed through the dangerous dark
Back alleys of the derelict estate!

Fear is a predator cornering off a small helpless
Animal and you hearing its horrified last scream
For help and wondering if you're dessert.

Fear is sound that chills and tingles your bones
And makes you tremble with fear.

Scott David Thomas (13)
Pen-Y-Dre High School

FEAR

Fear is seeing someone peering through your door with eyes looking
like a volcano has just erupted in his eyes and your spine is turning
into ice.
Fear is being chased by a mental patient that has escaped from a
psychiatric prison and he's trying to kill you.
Fear is walking through a forest of total darkness and hearing
blood-curdling howls coming from all around you,
And you're so scared you can't even move and you're afraid you're
going to be eaten alive.

Fear is waking up in the morning and everyone has disappeared.
Everywhere you walk you can see blood-red eyes peering from
everywhere you look.
Fear is being locked in a morgue with loads of bodies and wall to wall
deadly shadows of people but there is nobody there.

Matthew Patrick (13)
Pen-Y-Dre High School

FEAR

Owls swooping in the night under the dark canopy of the forest,
Wild animals howling, screaming, sending shivers up your spine
Looking at you with their beady little eyes.
Lions roaring it's like a sudden burst of thunder.
Spiders with legs like a pencil so thin and hairy
As they climb up your leg.
Foxes so cunning as they sneak around
Trying to find some prey.
Alligators so sneaking as they lurk in the
Muddy swamps.

Gavin Williams (13)
Pen-Y-Dre High School

FEAR IS... WHAT FEAR DOES...

Fear of walking down a dark street,
Eyes wide open staring at your feet,
A sudden noise in the night,
A loud bang, you freeze with fright,
Fear tells you to quicken your pace,
A whistling wind from outer space,
Fear grips you like a shark,
It won't let go because it's dark,
My heart is pounding like a drum,
I want it to stop I feel so numb,
Fear is what you think,
Fear takes your imagination to the brink,
Fear is scary you just can't win,
Fear is injected into your adrenaline...

Jonathan Sims (13)
Pen-Y-Dre High School

VAMP BEAR TEACHER

My name is Vamp Bear Teacher
I have 24 toes
A bear's body
And a very runny nose.
I smell like cheesy feet and
Like all things I eat.
My favourite food is little children
With sugar on top.
I gobble them
And they go down with a pop.

Lyndsey Smith (12)
Pen-Y-Dre High School

SPITTING FAT DEVIL

I have horns as arms
And teeth like sharp razor blades
I have fire as eyes
And I rip flesh apart
With my long red devil's tail.

My name is Spitting Fat Devil
I weigh one thousand pounds.
My head is a volcano
And I make loads of weird sounds.

I drink blood every day
And I love being mad
I smell like petrol and rotten socks
And my mother is so glad.

Jennifer Price (12)
Pen-Y-Dre High School

NIGHT-TIME

Night-time is a scary time full of sounds and smells
You cannot distinguish,
The clock's constant tick tocks that send ice-cold
Shivers down my spine
And car engines revving up as if in a race,
Hail showering houses like the hammering of machine gun fire
And the sound of someone creeping along, the long
And lonely hallway.
The wind whistling through the window
And the dark curtains swaying in the wind.

Gareth French (12)
Pen-Y-Dre High School

THE SOUNDS OF A STORM

The sound of a werewolf howling
The sound of crashing waves
The sound of a tapping at the door
It's all because of the storm.

The sound of a silent predator
The sound of an army stampeding through the eerie skies.
The sound of a million beads hitting a hard floor
It's all because of the storm.

As the storm dies away
The sounds calm to silence
Now all that remains is
The destruction of such violence.

Jenny Jones (13)
Pen-Y-Dre High School

WELSH RUGBY

Wales are great
Wales are such fun
We've got the Millennium Stadium
We love it when we win
We hate it when we lose.
When we win a match, we celebrate with booze.
New Zealand team are so fat
England are so thin.
When we win a match we tear them
Limb from limb

Richard Jones (13)
Pen-Y-Dre High School

MYSELF POEM

I am as handsome as a prince
As clever as old Mac Don
As clean as a baby's bottom
As strong as a bud of cotton.

I am as ugly as a duck
As thick as a brick
As dirty as pig
As weak as China.

As strong as a cup of tea
As strong as the Welsh team
As black as night
As clear as day.

James Thomas (12)
Pen-Y-Dre High School

NIGHT-TIME

The wind was whistling, whining, swaying the trees,
The clock ticking away as you restlessly recline in your bed,
Thunder and lightning bashing like waves against the rocks,
Shadows crawl silently across the eerie, slippery floor,
The animals screech, hoot and bark in a peaceful silent evening,
Creaking wooden floorboards reoccurring very loudly.
Peaceful dreams will stay forever in your mind,
Dark is black, frightening and deathly quiet,
Sounds of night are loud, quiet and suddenly
Night-time is terrifying or brilliant.

Kirstie James (12)
Pen-Y-Dre High School

THE OLD MAN

All alone he sits at home.
The old man looks like a garden gnome,
With beard of grey and nose bright red,
He wonders, when will he be dead?
With memories of his beloved wife,
How much he's enjoyed his long life.
With a family his son's full grown,
Never mind his father who's on his own.
He bought a dog and named him Spark
Now he spends his time at the local park.
He reads a paper sitting on a bench,
Then down the pub, a thirst to quench.
He meets some old folk they begin to talk,
'Thanks Bill, mine's a Bacardi and Coke.'
They begin to chat about old times,
Digging coal down the mines.
Time to go home, it's time for sleep
Hoping he doesn't have to count sheep.
Dreams of life when he was young
Sitting on his allotment in the sun.
Wonder what will tomorrow bring?
For this old man the angels sing.

Michael Williams (11)
Pen-Y-Dre High School

THE MIND IN AN UNMADE BED

The blanket of midnight unfolds itself,
Spreads over my head and covers my eyes.
But my eyes are not shut
Like blue marbles . . . They gaze and focus
Fixating on nothing
Thinking of everything
Darting
Trying to concentrate.
It seems there is somewhere to run
Yet nowhere to hide.
I'm much too far away . . . So close to home,
The frustrations turns to desperate fear.
Where deep-rooted nerves grow anxious,
Crave for sunlight
Long for morning,
Clutching at the hands of time
Begging for mercy on weakened knees.
Time remains remorseless, stands firm
Imprisons the mind in an unmade bed
Where eternity is the present
Dreams are the past
Nightmares are the future.

Rebecca Meade (17)
Pen-Y-Dre High School

THE CHANGE IN THE WEATHER

The sun smiles on a happy morning
The people awake to a happy day
The world seems a happier place
As the children get ready to go and play.

The sun shines down in all its glory
But the Weatherman's telling a different story.
A cloud appears, a tell-tale sign
The rain will come - it's just a matter of time!

The first drops of rain start to fall
The children are no longer kicking the ball
They're in the house all comfortable and warm,
. . . Waiting till dawn.

Alex Morgans (13)
Pen-Y-Dre High School

NIGHT-TIME

The wooden floorboards creaking in the dark like an old rusty horse.
The sound of the old car driving down the long narrow road.
The old brown doors squeaking like a little brown mouse.
The thick rain lashing very hard against the window.
The cold wind blowing through the open window sending shivers down
my spine.
The loud ticking of the clock going back and forth like a big old brown
grandfather clock.
The black shadow of a tree looking like a big monster lurking
behind you.

Shalleena Mall (12)
Pen-Y-Dre High School

SHARK HUNT

Shark is a
Ferocious creature.
He glides through
The water,
An animal comes near,
Ragged teeth start to show,
Keep away.

He rolls back his eyes,
Unlikely to get away
Now the fish are game
The poor fish are
Never to be seen again.

Charlotte Abraham (14)
Pen-Y-Dre High School

FEAR

Fear is the long hairy legs and body of a
spider scuttling across the floor.

Fear is the creaking sounds of a floorboard
creaking in the old spooky house.

Fear is the loud banging sounds coming from the basement.
Fear is the sounds of screaming coming from the dark alleys.
Fear is the footsteps in the cemetery.
Fear is the spooky voices coming form the haunted house.
Fear is the wind blowing on the door.

Denise Mahoney (13)
Pen-Y-Dre High School

A POEM ABOUT WALES

Cymraeg!
Welsh rugby . . . It's not one man, it's a team.
It's about the blood that runs through the heart.
and your heart was beating when Gibbs scored that fantastic try
to beat England 32-31.
And then that feeling that Wales had won
Screaming and shouting with joy.

Cymraeg!
Now it's started again - the World Cup
And your heart starts jumping with excitement
as Wales walk out onto the pitch.
It's a feeling no one can describe.

Cymraeg!
And if we come to face the mighty All Blacks,
I have faith that Wales will win.
And what courage Wales must have to
face the mighty All Blacks.

To win - it must come from the heart, the mind and the guts.
What guts must Jason Jones Hughes have to face big John Lomu.
But will Wales win?
Well! I think they will!

Cymraeg!

Rhys Scrivens (12)
Pen-Y-Dre High School

RUGBY

Graham Henry is his name,
Coaching Wales is his game.
We beat England 32-31
Scotland won the Five Nations,
It's over and done!

The Racecourse hosted Samoa-v-Japan
They all screamed Somoa! All except one fan
Somoa had the victory -
So all the Japanese decided to flee.

Then England beat Italy,
'I'm not happy at all!' said me.
Lawrence Dallaglio played in this game,
A few months ago he lost his fame.

Neil Jenkins is the greatest kicker of all time,
When he scores in a Welsh match, he shines.
He gets the ball between the posts -
'Look at that ball as it floats!'

We only wish that Wales could win the Rugby World Cup
Then Wales will be moving on up.
'Come on Wales!' we all cheered
And if we do win . . .
All the Welsh will be down the pub for a beer!

Robert Phillips (13)
Pen-Y-Dre High School

WEAK

I am as weak as an estranged cry for help
An endangered animal's dying yelp
As weak as a woman is to a man
Or the competition between boring and fun.

I'm as weak as a newborn baby's cry
An asthmatic person's frustrated sigh
As weak as a patient in a hospital bed
Or a Jurassic dinosaur's preserved head.

I am as weak as the liquidy sun that does rise
And the obviousness in a fraud's lies
As weak as a bird who's missing a wing
Or a popstar who just cannot sing.

Kirsty Purnell (12)
Pen-Y-Dre High School

A FROZEN HUMAN

As you fell onto a grass bank you froze like an iceberg
as the bridge swung over the tip of the grass blades,
the water dripped on the tip of a leaf.

As a sheet of white silk which looked like a
clear piece of ice on the grass blade swayed in the frosty wind.
You lay beside, as the water fell onto the tip of your finger, you pressed
the rain drop onto your tongue, I gasped and fell onto the frosty grass.
The grass grew as you lay there frozen with sadness, your blue eyes
flickered, a raindrop dropped and you crept up to the wall as the sun
rose, the ice melted and you became alive again.

Kelly Phillips & Kristie Abbruzzese (11)
Pen-Y-Dre High School

ACROSS THE OCEAN

I was sailing across the ocean in my boat
where the weather is strong and the sea is cold.
Heading towards the island of Salu
thinking of my future - where the sky is blue.
All of a sudden I came to a wall
a wall that was very tall.
Over the wall was my future holiday.
But with luck I saw a hole
a hole that was big enough for my boat.
As I got past the wall
I came to the island of Salu
where the sun is shining and the
sky is blue.

Carwyn Evans (14)
Pen-Y-Dre High School

RUGBY WORLD CUP

Wales is playing Argentina today
in the Rugby World Cup.
Screaming and shouting fans
were
hissing when they're hit.
It would be a privilege to
see them play.
A great place to be.
The Rugby World Cup is an honour.
To hear them say they've won.
Every fan of Wales . . . Is happy.

Sian Lewis (13)
Pen-Y-Dre High School

HENRY THE VIII

Bluff King Hal was full of beans;
He married half a dozen queens.
For three called Kate they cried the banns
And one called Jane and a couple of Annes.

The first he asked to share his reign
Was Kate of Aragon, straight from Spain.
But when his love for her was spent
He got a divorce, and out she went.

Anne Boleyn was his second wife
He swore to cherish her all his life.
But seeing a third, he wished instead,
He chopped off poor Anne Boleyn's head!

Alex Davies (12)
Pen-Y-Dre High School

FEAR IS . . .

Fear is walking alone down a dark lonely alley with no one there
just sounds of the wind whistling through the bushes and trees.
Fear is cars whizzing past you at night when you're alone on a
motorway with no one there to help you.
Fear is any dark lonely place where there is no light, only the cars
passing with their headlights flickering across the dark cold stone floor.
Fear is walking through an old creepy house with cobwebs everywhere,
no lights to guide you, nobody to talk to.
You're all alone in an old creepy house.
Fear is a big black hairy spider right in front of your bare little foot.
The spider slowly scuttles up on your foot and up your trouser leg.
Fear is the worst emotion invented.

Anna Davies (13)
Pen-Y-Dre High School

MILLENNIUM STADIUM

Friday the first at 3 o'clock,
The singing starts, it may never stop.
Hoisted into the air is that great oval ball
To be one of the crowd I'd give my all.

The Millennium Stadium open at last,
75,000 people, they look quite a cast.
As Neil Jenkins kicks the ball,
We all hope it will lead to a goal.

We'll see off the Argies,
We'll see off the rest,
Because we are Welsh,
We know we are the best.

Melanie Hier (13)
Pen-Y-Dre High School

WALES

We have a great tradition,
Our tradition is being Welsh.
When we walk across the hills,
All we hear is *squelsh!*

We have a load of valleys
Covered with daffodils and sheep,
If you look down one of our coalmines,
You can see they are quite deep!

There's one more thing that I can say,
I'm so proud to be Welsh!

Emma Kennedy (14)
Pen-Y-Dre High School

THE STORM

A roar of thunder
A flash of lightning
The rain comes pouring
And the wind is howling.

The noise is deafening
The light is blinding
The water is rising
And the howl is damaging.

A storm is brewing
There's more to come
The waves are crashing
And the sky is dull.

Roofs are leaking
The windows are shaking
Blinded with fear
And the noise is deafening.

All through the night
It carries on
Louder and stronger
The damage goes on.

It's early morning
And the storm has gone
Damaged for life
For that fearful night.

Laura Howley (13)
Pen-Y-Dre High School

FEAR

Dogs barking in the old kennel
the bark is noisy and the tone
goes through me.

Owls howling in the deserted forest
blood-curdling owls and a creepy forest.

A spider crawling up my arm
pulling off all the hair as it crawls along.

A bull running flat out towards you
with great strength about him.

Fear is Jonah Lomu flatting me out
as he pulls me down and
snatches the rugby ball out of my hands.

Fear is someone tapping me on
the shoulder and me turning round
and someone holding a gun to my head.

Fear is when you are alone in
the house and the floorboards
are creaking late at night.

Fear is when you are alone in
the house and one of the windows
open and the strength of the
wind slams the door.

David Jones (13)
Pen-Y-Dre High School

THE CAVE AHEAD

I am standing in a boat
going across the sea.
The weather is very hot,
the view is outstanding.
The mountains are very big
and the sea is blue-green.
As I carry on steering
I come to something big.
A black net with buoys
floating on the top.

I struggle and struggle
and try and try
to get by the big black net.
So I get out a knife,
cut off the floating buoys.
The big black net sinks
to the bottom of the blue-green sea.
So that was my fantasy . . .

I made my way up to the cave
to see what I could see -
until I came to the entrance.
I go to the entrance
and my eyes open wide
because I had a shock
by loads of rocks . . .
Blocking the way in!

Leanne Hughes (14)
Pen-Y-Dre High School

THE GRADUAL CHANGE!

I'm in my bed all comfortable and warm
And then I realise the curtains are drawn.
I tuck my head back under my pillows
And then I await for the cows to bellow.

I can't get out of my tormenting bed,
It feels that if my legs are dead.
I try and get up but my legs are aching
And down the stairs my breakfast's awaiting.

I look out the door and there I'm glaring
And then I see the sun is blaring
And there I see the cart of the milkman
My breakfast awaits, so I had to run.

It's 3.00 p.m. and I'm going out,
I'll play with the footy, as if there's a doubt,
From up above flies down a feather,
The game is spoiled by only the weather.

I'm getting bored, I need to be occupied,
It's now boring, it's like someone died,
I grab the controller and put on the telly
I'm getting hungry, I need to fill my belly.

It's getting dark and I want to relax
The footy's on now just sit back
But before I do I would like to say
That I think today, was a gradual change.

Scott Vaughan (13)
Pen-Y-Dre High School

TV

TV is what we talk about
Every day and night
Whether it's a wedding
Or a nasty, bloody fight!
Eastenders, Brookie
and all the rest.
Corrie, Neighbours
Which is the best?
We can visit Pobl Y Cwm
for a drink in the Deri.
Or turn to the Springer Show
and watch them shout 'Jerry!'
We also hear worldwide news
some of it bad
From the death of Diana
to some poor lad!
Characters we all remember
who scream, fight and
camp out all night
are Bianca, Grant and Spider.
Cookery programmes show
how to make a crumpet.
What really gets on our nerves
is Sonia and her trumpet!
We all feel sorry for
poor Matthew in jail
but what we really want
is a new hairdo for Gail!

Caitlin McBride (13)
Pen-Y-Dre High School

THE DEADLY FOG

It starts
as a misty haze
as alone in the house
the fire does blaze

I sit in my old
rocking chair
as the mist silently
sneaks up through the air

Then as the mist thickens
there's a chill through the sky
I see the fog coming
I scream out and cry

The fog is hungry
it looks for its prey.
I feel it coming
in the house - I won't stay

I run through the back door
and hide in the tree
I see the fog coming
it's coming for me

Suddenly it goes silent
I see a light
I try to reach it
through the thick trees I fight.

I try to keep running
but I fall to the floor
The dark blanket covers me
and I am no more

Donna Williams (14)
Pen-Y-Dre High School

FIFTH ELEMENT

F   our precious stones and the fifth element,
I   ncreasingly outnumbered, the odds are not good.
F   ive brave people all believe
T   hey can save the planet and live out its creed,
H   old on to the stones, or they may slip.

E   arth, fire, wind, rain in your grip,
L   ove is the only key to success,
E   normous powers will do the rest,
M   illions of lives here at stake,
E   very being starting to shake,
N   ick of time, the force is hurled,
T   ogether they did it, they saved the world.

Simon Miles (13)
Pen-Y-Dre High School

SNOW

It falls from the sky with
patience and skill.
Dances and prances
on the midday breeze.
Then covers the ground
with the softest of touch.
With such a calm fall
it cools the breeze.
It does not stampede or clash
with the breeze.
It just floats with its calm
and tender needs.

Beth Rosser (13)
Pen-Y-Dre High School

SHOPS

There are some shops that open,
There are some shops that close.
Some shops have windows,
All shops have doors.

There are some shops that open 24 hours a day,
But they don't get much money,
So the assistants don't get much pay.

Second-hand goods, groceries too,
Even things to decorate your room.
Shops with jewellery, diamond rings,
Who knows what the next shop could bring?

Hannah Evans (13)
Pen-Y-Dre High School

STEREOPHONICS

They made a song about rugby
They sung a song about traffic.
They come from Cwmaman
Where they started off slow
Their baby-faced singer
And a mad man drummer
Their bassist Richard with his tattoos galore.
Richard, Stuart and Kelly are the Stereophonics,
With their hit *Bartender and the Thief!*
Two awards that they have won.
They are the Sterophonics
And they're my *number one!*

Gemma Hughes (13)
Pen-Y-Dre High School

JOE

I once knew a man his name was Joe
He lived in his house all on his own.
He had no friends, just a cat, black and scruffy
it looked like a rat.
His house was old and very small, it's a wonder
he could fit in there at all.
His clothes were torn, dirty and damp.
He begged on the streets just like a tramp.
One day I knocked at his door, there was no answer
so I knocked some more.
I walked round the back, his door was ajar.
I tiptoed in, but not very far.
His cat jumped and I fell back
One of his plates fell *crack!*
I quickly got up and turned around
I went to go home but I heard a sound.
I walked in the living room and all I saw
was an old man knocked out on the floor.
An ambulance came and took him away,
when he recovered he had a place to stay.
They found him a house, dry and clean,
on a council estate where no one was mean.
He found some friends and a wife.
He lived happily ever after
for the rest of his life.

Nicky Jones (13)
Pen-Y-Dre High School

DOLPHINS POEM

Dolphins are friendly with nearly everyone.
Some people try to shoot them with a gun
They go in herds to catch their food
Bottle-nosed you can have
They can give you lots of love.
Just like two turtle doves.
I love them very much
They are wonderful to touch.
They can be entertaining
Even when it's raining.
They are cute and friendly too
You might find them in a zoo.
Seas and oceans they do live
They make you look like a div.
Some of them become fish portions
If you find them in the oceans.
They are grey and white,
You might see them in the night.
If you want to see their tummy
Don't be tight and spend your money.
They blow water in the air
They might do it in a pair.
They have very little eyes
These also make me cry.
I can jump everywhere
When you look . . . I am there!

Lisa Marie Binks (12)
Pen-Y-Dre High School

ALONE!

The night is dark,
I sit on my own,
I'm freezing cold
And I'm all alone.

My hair is matted,
My feet are bare,
I have no money,
No clean clothes to wear!

I think of my family
In a warm home,
Their stomachs are full,
But starving I roam.

I cannot buy anything,
I'll have to steal
From a market stall or shop,
Just to have a meal.

Heartache and pain
Is what I feel.
Is it a dream
Or is it real?

The night is still dark,
I sit on my own,
I'm freezing cold
And I'm all alone!

Samantha Taylor (13)
Pen-Y-Dre High School

A LONG JOURNEY

I'm travelling in a car
I'm driving on the motorway
Heading for a long journey.
It's a cold and miserable day.
Traffic lights and cars everywhere.
I'm looking out of the car window.
I see muddy fields and no animals.

I'm thinking what is ahead of me
Sunny peaceful days
Animals in lush green fields
Cool rivers which illuminate the dark.

I'm distracted by cars and people talking
I then look ahead.
I can see big high mountains
They are close and tight together
They are blocking me!

I can't get through
I can't go round
I think where I'm going . . .
Is trapped behind the mountains!

Kelly Thomas (14)
Pen-Y-Dre High School

TEARS FOR TRAGEDIES

The world carries on, oblivious to the tragedies occurring.
People are murdered, robbed of their life, dying of old age
or natural causes,
People grieve, cry or they sometimes bottle up their feelings,
Holding their emotions back, not wanting to show how they feel.
When people or pets pass away, their relatives or friends
Sometimes cry, letting themselves go.
Tears stream down their faces like a never-ending waterfall,
Not knowing what to do or say.
Alone in the night, rocking back and forth,
Crying - distressed - tears.
Tears for death,
Tears for the loss of life,
Tears for tragedies.

Simone Morris (13)
Pontarddulais Comprehensive School

CASTELL-COCH

A red-orange glow in the windows,
A cheery castle - red in colour,
Shining on its mountain of trees,
Shrouded in myth.
Inside lies a room
Filled with a beauty so deep
With its mischievous fairies
Dancing in the candle light.
A warm, golden aura filling the coldest of hearts,
A Welsh castle in a pine forest
Capturing your mind with memories.

Kaity Lee (13)
Pontarddulais Comprehensive School

WALES

Wales is a Welsh valley of song,
Pits and coalminers are now long gone.
Men worked long and hard underground,
Many pits closed, few are around.

Voices are heard in hills and dales,
Choirs galore, but mostly males.
Poets and songsters, listen, hark,
Melodies played with a harp.

March the 1st, it's St David's Day
And everyone has a great ball.
Costumes, Welsh leeks and daffodils
Celebrated by one and all.

On the beaches along the seashore,
People pick cockles, 'Alive, alive oh,'
Gather seaweed, make lava bread,
Very high in iron, or so it's said.

Old castles stand so bold and high,
The Welsh flag flies high in the sky,
The dragon breathes its flames so red,
No, our Welsh heritage is not dead.

Julie Anthony (12)
Pontarddulais Comprehensive School

THE LAUNCH

It is the launch,
Ten, nine, eight, seven, six,
Everybody's watching,
Will USA get there first?
Watch the launch to find out.

The launch has begun,
Five, four, three, two, one, blast off!
Everybody's shouting
As the shuttle goes up,
Now you've seen it,
You've watched the launch.

Matthew Brooks (12)
Pontarddulais Comprehensive School

SUMMER SUN

Summer sun,
Sand and sea,
Summer sun,
It shines on me.

Summer sun,
It shines in St Cyp,
Summer sun,
Like a golden drip.

Summer sun,
High above the hall,
Summer sun,
Now it starts to fall.

Summer sun
It falls over sea,
Summer sun,
Everyone is happy.

Summer sun,
Sand and sea,
Summer sun,
It shone on me.

Robert Barnes (12)
Pontarddulais Comprehensive School

THE DARK

The dark is cold,
The dark is scary,
The clock strikes eight,
Time for bed.
The dark.
I hide under my quilt,
I'm scared of the dark,
I have a light on,
A fly comes on the light,
The shadow is big,
So I scream.
In the dark, a monster comes from under my bed,
It is horrible, I'm afraid.
Help!
The dark is dangerous,
The dark is creepy.
Help! The dark!

Laura Doidge (12)
Pontarddulais Comprehensive School

THE ROLLER-COASTER

It is seen at a distance,
soaring high into the sky,
only still for a moment,
until something whizzes by.

Clicks and chains that rattle on,
screams that echo in the air,
knuckles white and teeth clenching,
panic-stricken faces everywhere.

Can I get off? It's too late.
Sitting there in the front seat,
rising slowly up to heaven,
can't believe this is a treat!

Reach the top, just look and stare,
over the sea and high land,
I'm going down through the air,
I hope I don't hit the sand.

Rachael Flanagan (12)
Pontarddulais Comprehensive School

I WONDER, I WONDER

I wonder what is beyond the stars,
Jupiter, Venus, Pluto and Mars.

Rockets fly to planets and to the moon,
Will we go further and further too soon?

I wonder what is beyond the stars,
Jupiter, Venus, Pluto and Mars.

We are mere specks in the universe,
Perhaps we are here because of a curse.

I wonder what is beyond the stars,
Jupiter, Venus, Pluto and Mars.

Maybe a meteorite will crash down to Earth
We must stay calm, to prove our worth.

I wonder what is beyond the stars,
Jupiter, Venus, Pluto and Mars.

Zoe Charlotte Lewis (12)
Pontarddulais Comprehensive School

THE SEASONS

Springtime.
Newborn lambs gambol high,
Clouds begin to leave the sky,
Easter rabbit, chocolate eggs,
Cider from an open keg.
Palms and crosses, crucifixion,
Hope and glory,
Resurrection.

Summertime.
No more rain, now it's dry,
Sun shines bright in the sky,
Warm, hot summer, suntan cream,
Holidays are not a dream.
Sun and seaside, exclamations,
Joy and cheer,
Birthday girl time.

Autumn time.
Crunching leaves on the floor,
Smell of pine comes through the door,
Cold, harsh breeze, my toes freeze.
Beauty lies within the trees,
Green and red-brown, colourations.
Nice hot soup,
As I go in.

Wintertime.
Snow falls in wintertime,
Ice and rain also come,
It's so cold I get a chill,

Frozen trees look stiff and still,
Leaves and acorns, decorations,
The time has come,
Christmas Day.

Sophie Lewis (11)
Pontarddulais Comprehensive School

LARRY THE LIZARD

Larry the lanky lizard
Lazes around all day
Larry the lanky lizard
Lures his poor prey

Larry the lanky lizard
Sometimes likes to play
But Larry the lizard
Prefers to laze all day

Larry the loopy lizard
Who is long, lovely and lanky
But when he goes to discos
He does the Hanky Panky

Larry the lanky lizard
Who is long and green
He has a large green tail
And he looks like a bean

Larry the lanky lizard
Loves his bed of hay
But Larry the lizard
Prefers to laze all day.

Thomas Burgess (12)
Pontarddulais Comprehensive School

NIGHTMARES

Up I bolted,
Totally scared stiff,
Shivering cold,
A little bit miffed.

Tears were running,
My throat very dry,
Why did it start,
Oh please tell me why?

What did it mean?
Why was she there?
Murdering people
With that nasty stare.

Nothing like her,
She was always nice,
She seemed different,
Cold and sharp as ice.

How did she kill
Those poor and sad souls?
Sliced through their hearts
Like some destined goal.

It must make sense,
It was just a dream,
Deep and absurd,
That heart-tearing scene.

Emily Dawson (12)
Pontarddulais Comprehensive School

ANGELS

Their hair is soft, as soft as snow.
A gold halo shining above their heads.
With a pure white dress and delicate wings,
Angels that fly in the sky,
Angels that fly on the wind.

Making dreams come true,
They chant at night.
When you sleep they're always here,
Don't be afraid, they are near,
Watching over you with lots of love,
Your guardian angels from above.

Flying high into the sky,
Looking down on you,
Making sure you're okay
Angels that fly in the sky,
Angels that fly on the wind.

Playing their trumpets as they fly along,
Playing a happy tune.
Singing and dancing to the sweet music.
Watching you, every move you make.
Angels with shiny gold halos,
Angels with delicate wings.

Their hair is soft, as soft as snow.
A gold halo shining above their heads.
With a pure white dress and delicate wings,
Angels that fly in the sky,
Angels that fly on the wind.

Emma Caie (12)
Pontarddulais Comprehensive School

SPRING

The early morning when the sun comes up
The lambs are prancing about.
The chicks all fluffy and yellow
Where cows are feeding off their mother.
Horses and their babies galloping about
And the farmer has just woken up.

The flowers are bright and beautiful
Bees working hard all day
To make honey for their owners.
Children swimming in their swimming pools
Little birds singing all day.

People sunbathing down on the beach
Beautiful butterflies fluttering about
Big towering trees with their big green leaves
Fish swimming around in the big blue sea
Barbecue smells everywhere you go.

You don't know what's going to happen this year
You are not going to need your woolly clothing.
All you are going to need is your shorts
The clouds are fluffy and white.

The sun shining bright
And the ice-cream man is very busy.
No one is in which is lucky
Because the mums can have a cup of coffee.

The spiders won't go hungry
Because the flies are in all spring and summer.
At night when all is quiet
And people in bed all snug and tight
There's another spring day tomorrow
Where fun and laughter starts all over again.

Charlotte Sanders (11)
Pontarddulais Comprehensive School

THE SEASIDE

People using suntan cream
People bathing by the sea
Other people scream and shout
Little children run about.

Seagulls singing in the sky
The sun beaming on the beach
People swimming in the sea
People run along the sand.

Dead fish floating in the sea
Sewage floating past my knee
Jellyfish stinging people
Lots of crabs crawling around.

Sand in people's sandwiches
Salt in everybody's mouth
Eating hot dogs on the beach
Listening to radios.

It is now time to go home
But nobody wants to leave
They'd rather stay at the beach
And enjoy the nice sea breeze.

Angharad Evans (13)
Pontarddulais Comprehensive School

THE LONELY LITTLE GIRL
(Dedicated to the story of the little matchstick girl)

Sitting in the corner,
As quiet as a mouse,
A lonely little Welsh girl,
Who weeps away her life.

A family which despise her,
A mother who beats her,
A father who doesn't want her,
Where does that leave her now?

A brother who kicks her,
A sister who hits her,
A sad brutal and violent life,
With no one who cares in sight.

She's always neglected,
A mysterious child,
Full of wonders and dreams,
Which she wants to come true.

The day will come when she will be free,
The loneliness will leave her,
And will all wash away,
The day will be tomorrow, let's hope and pray.

Rachel Powell (12)
Pontarddulais Comprehensive School

AUTUMN

Leaves fell from the trees,
Swirling and swaying away.
Brown leaves,
Dark green leaves,
Dead branches,
All fell off the trees.

Birds' nests fell apart,
Kids started playing with the leaves.
It started to rain,
Autumn was ending,
Winter was soon to come.

Emma Morris (11)
Pontarddulais Comprehensive School

FAMILY, WHO NEEDS THEM?

I don't need my brother,
All noisy and messy.
He's a little horror,
According to my mother.

I don't need my sisters,
All bossy and ancient.
Their creepy little lives,
Giving me mind twisters.

I don't need my mother,
Who's cleaning up the house.
Always bossing me about,
Screaming at my brother.

I don't need my father,
Watching boring programmes.
Saying 'The good old days,'
Making me like my mother.

Most of all I don't need my dog,
Barking all night long.
Losing her hair on clothes,
Slobbering on next door's mog.

Linda Taylor (13)
Pontarddulais Comprehensive School

SHOPPING

I shop a lot
I shop till I drop
I can never stop
I live to shop

I shop in Miss Selfridges
Tammy and Clairs
I buy shoes and clothes
And clips for my hair

I've bought loads and loads of things
Like glittery tops and shiny rings
I always buy lots of stuff
Sometimes I don't have enough

Sometimes I buy something nice
If my friends asked me, I wouldn't think twice
I go shopping every chance I get
I'll come home with no money I bet

Shopping really is cool
I sometimes go after school
I don't know why boys don't like it
They only buy a new football kit.

Angela Brugnoli (12)
Pontarddulais Comprehensive School

CHRISTMASTIME

On Christmas Eve I was lying on my bed,
Waiting for Santa to come down the chimney.
I lay and waited patiently asking myself 'Is he ever going to come?'
How's he going to get down,
My chimney's pretty narrow,
And he's obviously chubby like everyone says.

I've been waiting six months for my BMX,
Because my other one broke in the summer.
I wait in silence in my lonely room,
Only the sound of heavy snow,
As I hear munching of cookies and slurping of milk,
I run downstairs and see Santa going up the chimney.

James Miles (11)
Pontarddulais Comprehensive School

MY FAMILY FOOTBALL TEAM

My brother's in goal
Dad's in defence
Mum's in midfield
And gran's on the bench.

I am centre-forward
Uncle Elvet's at the back
My niece is the manager
But my cousin's in attack.

Aunty Sue is our coach
Just because I missed
An open goal last week
I'm on the transfer list.

We are bottom of our League
And cannot score a goal
Our family football team
Is in a bit of a hole.

I got sent off
And my dad got booked
I'm suspended for three matches
Our fans can't look!

Richard Price (13)
Pontarddulais Comprehensive School

FEARS

Some people are scared of spiders
Daddy-long-legs, tarantulas and black widows
Fat ones, skinny ones, hairy ones, bald ones
Deadly ones, harmless ones
Arachnophobia - fear of spiders

Some people are scared of small spaces
Lifts, cars, cupboards, closets, changing rooms, toilet cubicles
Claustrophobia - fear of small spaces

Some people are scared of heights
Cliffs, the Eiffel Tower, Everest,
Nemesis, The Bounce, Snowdon, Oblivion
Pepsi Max
Vertigo - fear of heights

Some people are scared of big spaces
Shops, supermarkets, schools, churches
Amusement parks, the great outdoors
Agoraphobia - fear of open spaces

Some people are scared of dentists
The dentist's chair, rubber gloves, drills
Anaesthetic, fillings, braces
Dentaphobia - fear of dentists!

Amber Carlisle (13)
Pontarddulais Comprehensive School

MAGIC

'Abracadabra!' shouted the magician
As the black rabbit dropped into the hat,
'A wave with my wand,' he cried with delight,
As the rabbit came out as a cat.

'Abracadabra!' shouted the magician,
As the black cat was dropped into the hat.
'A wave with my wand,' he cried with delight,
As the cat came out as a rabbit.

Alex Sutton (11)
Pontarddulais Comprehensive School

WHAT IS A STAR?

What is a star?
A wild nuclear reaction?
Or is it
God's gift to voyagers, guiding them on their quests?

What is a star?
A cloud of bubbling acid?
Or is it
A raging firework burning with scarlet and crimson flames?

What is a star?
A burst of poisonous gases?
Or is it
The eyes of a predator stalking the planet Earth?

What is a star?
A cluster of violent atoms?
Or is it
A streetlight on the road to God's palace?

What is a star?
A heat rash of light?
Or is it
God's guide's torchlight showing the way to heaven?
Who knows?

Lewis Evans (11)
Pontarddulais Comprehensive School

AT THE SEASIDE

On the seaside we will play.
Listen to the children
Look at the faces gleaming.
Hear the children screaming.
Kites flying high to the sky
Children go on crying
They could be very tired.

Hear the sounds of the seashore,
Look at the pretty shells.
Feel the squelch of the seaweed.
Watch out for the crabs pincers.
Sit on all the rocks around us.

Wow! So many children
Now it's time for them to go.
Now the stars are shining
Children's last shrieks of fun,
Day has turned to night.

Jasmine Kelly (13)
Pontarddulais Comprehensive School

BULLIES

I know of a bully,
She bullies me all day,
I think her name is Zoe,
The one I have to pay.

I know of a bully
Who is an awful pain,
She speaks awfully silly,
But she's never the same.

I know of a bully
Who hardly has a friend,
Except for one called Nilly,
Who's a friend till the end.

I know of a bully
And she gets on your nerves,
She takes your dinner money,
But never gets served.

Vicki Erasmus (12)
Pontarddulais Comprehensive School

A DERELICT CHURCH

The church stood out like a burning flame,
The storm made hundreds of clashing sounds,
And the gargoyles on the walls
Looked like demons.
I looked ahead to the entrance
And a shadowy figure stood there . . .

My body froze
And I stared,
Suddenly a smash of lightning
Took my eyes off the figure,
It started to rain.

I fell to my feet at another bolt of lightning
And I looked back to the entrance . . .
Nothing, no shadowy figure,
Then the clock struck ten,
The rain slowed down to a stop . . .

Then I heard a scream.

Rhodri Walters (11)
Pontarddulais Comprehensive School

THE MIDNIGHT SKY

The midnight sky on a good night,
is placid and starry.

Then a rapid blast of wind occurs,
and swirls the sky into a
mystical array of dull but starry adventure.

Unexpectedly it all relaxed down,
like there was no starry adventure,
no mystical array.

Shapes started forming out of the deep,
gloomy nothing.
Almost as if it's telling a story,
of deep, dark entrapment.

The shapes started disappearing
to the instinct, obscure beyond,
until it was how it started,
calm and starry.

Eluned Erasmus (12)
Pontarddulais Comprehensive School

DOLPHINS

Speeding across the blue bay,
Leaping through the foam,
Watch them swimming away,
Happy in their home.

They travel through the oceans,
Eating tasty fish,
A juicy mackerel portion,
Is their favourite dish.

All day long the sun shines bright,
On the rocks and isles,
The sleepy seals sit and watch
As they swim for miles.

Watching the bright sun go down,
They leap through the waves,
One of them acts like a clown,
Hiding in the cave.

Elinor Lewis (12)
Pontarddulais Comprehensive School

MY GREEN ELEPHANT

When I was small,
I had my first toy,
My first toy.
I took it everywhere with me,
In my pram I had three with me,
but I cuddled my green elephant.
In my cot I had ten with me.
But I cuddled my green elephant
I took it everywhere with me,
When I was 7 I had lost it.
I was sad for a bit,
but I got over it,
And when I was 9 at Christmastime,
I had a small soft pressie
and when I opened it,
it was my green elephant,
I was so happy,
And since then I cuddle it in
bed with me.

Linda Lewis (12)
Pontarddulais Comprehensive School

MILLENNIUM

This New Year's Eve
I will receive
Lots and lots of lager
I'll crash through the door
And fall on the floor
Just trying to be like my father

Everyone's cheering
And having a laugh
They all smell of booze
They all need a bath

We're at the Ritz
All the glamour and glitz
Celebrating the New Year in style
We'll party all night
Until the daylight
I'll remember this night
For quite a while.

Joanne Richards (13)
Pontarddulais Comprehensive School

FOX, FOX, FOX

Night, night, night,
As the fox comes out
With his big, bushy tail.
You'd better watch out.

Bright, bright, bright,
As the sun comes out
And the fox goes to bed
After a long night out.

Fright, fright, fright,
As you see him prowl
In the big, dark night
With his big, angry growl.

Tight, tight, tight,
Will he ever share,
As he sees his pray,
His big, juicy hare.

Joanne Sulsh (12)
Pontarddulais Comprehensive School

JUST A LITTLE GIRL

Just a little girl at the age of five
Parents arguing for the first time
Dad in a bad temper
Mum upset
Dad blames everybody except himself.

After a while they've calmed down
A couple of hours later they are off again
Throwing things,
Fighting,
But then comes Dad with his powerful
Fists and knocks my mum unconscious with a terrible blow.

I'll leave them arguing - I'll go
Upstairs, better things to do than
Listen to them
Shouting,
Bellowing,
I'll go and let the tarantulas, lizards and snakes out.

Natalie Adams (12)
Pontarddulais Comprehensive School

GRANDMA

I love Grandma,
She was loving and kind.
I love Grandma,
She was all mine.
Until one day she became very ill,
Grandma had to go to hospital.
I didn't want her to go.
I went to visit her once,
Her face was as white as snow,
'Please Grandma don't go!'
We walked into the church,
As silent as can be.
The music was playing,
People were sad but not as sad as me,
I love Grandma,
And she loves me.

Claire Anne McEwan (12)
Pontarddulais Comprehensive School

THE SEA

I like the sea
Crashing against the rocks
Calm in the sun
Heavy in the rain
Storms are coming
Lightning strikes
The sea is crashing against the rocks.

Thunder claps then it's gone, passed by
The sun is rising on the sea
Reflecting blue.

Natasha Lewis (12)
Pontarddulais Comprehensive School

WHERE NOBODY GOES

Dull, bold, grey and dark
Was everything about this house,
Vile, horrid and painful screams
Could be heard from the basement.

People who entered, never came back.
Werewolves could be heard
At 12 o'clock at night.
The doorsteps to the door each cracked and screamed.

Out like lost souls imprisoned,
The eyes of the statues and gargoyles.
Watch your every single move,
The trees around are bitter and horrid.

The door knocker is a shape like the devil's face,
With an evil grin that dominates you.

Stephen Drew (12)
Pontarddulais Comprehensive School

THE WITCHES

They come this time every year
It is the one night when the witches are raised from the dead
The witches are white with long noses
They wear long black funeral dresses
And black pointy hats, and they smell like frogs' breath
They haunt young children by hiding under their beds
They fly around the sky on their broomsticks
Looking for children to haunt
But when it strikes midnight they disappear
No one knows where
But we all know they will appear again next year.

Victoria Davies (13)
Pontarddulais Comprehensive School

THE CINEMA

You go to see films in the cinema
You sit down and watch the lights dim down.
You watch previews of new films coming soon
Star Wars, Austin Powers etcetera.

Some films are funny, some films are sad
And some are very very bad.
You sit there and watch, cry, laugh or snore,
Some films can be a complete utter bore.

Some films scare you and you bury your face,
In this dark, horrid - yet sacred place.
The big screen and sound will scare you silly,
You will say 'Oh, this place is the creeps!'

Some films are called *action* with shooting.
Lots with cops, some as dim as mops.
Others involve an army - eating salami
Special effects galore and some gore.

Overall - the cinema is tops!

Stuart Edwards (13)
Pontarddulais Comprehensive School

WINTER SNOW

Winter snow
Bright, but so deadly,
Winter snow
Comes down so heavily.

Winter snow
Will give you a fright,
Winter snow,
White and so bright.

Winter snow
Comes during the night,
Winter snow
Falls from a light.

Winter snow
Can sometimes be cool,
Winter snow
Turns to a pool.

Daniel Hurden (12)
Pontarddulais Comprehensive School

LOOK AT THE SEA

Look at the sea blue like the daylight sky.
Look at the children playing in
The golden sand on a summer's day.
Look at the sea calm as can be.
Look at the sea.

Look at the sea it's like a giant hand
Stroking the warm sand.
Look at the seaweed turning,
Swirling and whirling around in the waves.
Look at the sea as rough as can be.
Look at the sea.

Look at the dolphins
Playing with waves
Look at the fish swimming
Hoping to find some food.
Look at the dolphins as
Happy as can be.
Look at the sea.

Sarah Wassell (11)
Pontarddulais Comprehensive School

MOONY THE MAGICIAN

Moony the magician was a king
A very small king in fact
Which made it very awkward
When he performed his act

He had four servants to carry around
A magnifying glass so big and round
In order that his audience would see
What a clever magician the king could be

One day the king decided on a fantastic plan
To make himself a bigger man
He mixed up some potions
And lots of lotions
Said *'Abracadabra - abracadeye'*
In a puff of smoke he was twelve feet high

Now people come from far and wide
To see the king in all his pride
He is so happy for all to see
What a clever giant he can be.

Ceri Probert   (11)
Pontarddulais Comprehensive School

THREE ALIENS LIVE IN MY BEDROOM

Three aliens live in my bedroom,
Called Zippy, Zonker and Bob
When their spaceship crashed down in my garden,
The engine gave a last dying throb!

I sold the trashed ship for scrap metal,
The scrapyard bloke looked at me odd,
So I told him it was an old lampshade,
That had belonged to some rocker or mod!

Zippy is as thick as two short planks,
Zonker is really a bore
Bob is really quite clever mind
With him, homework's not a chore

Bob sometimes helps with my homework,
While Zippy just messes around,
But Zonker's a boring old jerk.
Uh oh, what's Zippy found?

Sam Batsford (12)
Pontarddulais Comprehensive School

WALES

Jenkins lines up to take the kick,
to convert the try scored by Gibbs
Jenkins runs up takes the kick
left a little, right a little.
Hallelujah it went in.

The Welsh players go mad
The English players go silent
The Welsh fans go crazy
The English fans go weeping

Quick as a flash
everyone got back to their positions
straight away Cat went for a dodgy drop kick.
Wembley went silent it came so close
Thank God he missed.

Now we go onto the World Cup
against Australia, South Africa and New Zealand,
will we win? Will we lose?
That my friend, time shall tell.

Ashley Draisey (12)
Pontarddulais Comprehensive School

TYPICAL TEENAGER'S ROOM!

Up in my mess here I am again
Hear my little sister call, she's a little pain.
Knock, knock! There's someone at the door.
My mother comes in as I chuck my skirt on the floor.
'Oh my God what hit this room!'
Nothing at all.
I stood by the door to see my mother's point of view.
'If you clean this up I'll buy you something new.'
All excited off I went but look what I had to clean up.
Only odd socks and mouldy milk,
Dresses, trousers, skirts made of silk.
Lipsticks, mascaras by Christian Dior
They should be in my make-up bag
And not all over the floor.
Smelly socks,
Old magazines,
Dirty trousers,
Cups of tea stuck to the table,
Plates and glasses from two weeks ago
My mess in a typical teenager's room!

Natalie Thomas
Pontarddulais Comprehensive School

MY DOG JOSIE

My dog is an idiot
She's also getting fat,
She eats apples from our garden
And chases next door's cat.

My dog is disobedient
But very, very cute,
She doesn't listen to a word you say
And doesn't give a hoot!

My dog is full of energy
She's busy all the time.
She runs up and down the garden
Getting caught in the washing line.

My dog gets excited
And does a little wee.
It really doesn't matter
Josie means the world to me.

Phillip White (11)
Pontarddulais Comprehensive School

OLD MOTHER HUBBARD

Old Mother Hubbard
Went to her cupboard
To fetch her dog a bone
But when she got there
The cupboard was bare
And so her dog had none.

She went to the baker's
To buy him some bread
But when she came back
Her poor dog was dead.

She went to the undertaker's
To buy him a coffin
But when she came back
The poor dog was laughin'

She took him a clean dish
To get him some tripe
But when she came back
He was smokin' a pipe.

Claire Gow (13)
Pontarddulais Comprehensive School

INDEPENDENT ME

I'm an independent girl
I do everything for myself
I am fourteen and a bit now
And I'm growing up really fast
Mum says go to bed by ten
But why can't I decide that?
She never lets me make my own decisions
And she treats me like a kid
My best friend Rebecca
Thinks I'm really cool
I do all the things
that she would never do
I suppose I better go now
And revise for my maths test
For when I get an A on that
I will simply be the best!

Amanda Robertson (13)
Pontarddulais Comprehensive School

DEEP, DARK NIGHT

A deep, dark night,
A rat squeaked and a cat miaowed,
The alley was dark and spooky.
The alley looked like it was disappearing in the distance.
As I walked down the alley,
I saw a shadow on the wall ahead.
The moon was full and I realised,
It was the shadow of the rustling trees,
That lined one side of the alley.

Mark Jason Ford (11)
Pontarddulais Comprehensive School

ONE DAY

One day when I wake up there will be peace,
One day when I walk down the road,
I will see mixed races bonding lovingly,
One day the word 'discrimination' will be extinct.
One day, the great American Civil War
Will be banished from the minds of all Americans.
One day, no hate will come of bad situations,
One day there will be no prejudice towards another,
One day, the definition of harmony will be
Simply the people around us.
One day, there will be no prisons,
One day the Protestants and Catholics will be
The epitome of friends.
One day, Caesar and Brutus's friendship will flower again,
One day people will walk unafraid,
One day . . .

Andrew Thomas (12)
Pontarddulais Comprehensive School

IN THE DEEP BLUE OCEAN

Deep in the ocean the fishes roam
As magical mermaids swim through the foam,
Sparkling oyster shells slowly unfold,
Revealing a pearl, white and so cold.
Crabs, eels and lobsters slowly swim by,
Then scurry through seaweed never to die,
Making the sand turn and wheel,
As light as air, as cool as sea
And wild and lazy as the sound
Of all that ocean all around.

Sarah Phelps (12)
Pontarddulais Comprehensive School

ALICE'S BEACH SHOP

Alice worked in a shop,
She worked in a beach shop.

Alice had a collection of shells,
Everyone bought shells.

She also sold ice-cream.
Every day people went to buy ice-cream.

On a hot summer's day she will go out,
She will go out to pick shells.

Alice liked working in her shop,
But she never liked picking shells.

When Alice goes out to the sea,
She never wants to come back.

Alice never does paddle in the sea,
Because she always swims.

She also went out to pick flowers,
Everyone went to buy flowers.

Cara Jayne George (11)
Pontarddulais Comprehensive School

ANIMALS

My name is Leo I am a lion,
I roar around the jungle,
When animals mess with me,
I swallow them down whole

My name is Alan I am an antelope,
I charge around at people,
When someone chases me I always get away,
But sometimes I get caught I get killed right away

I am a poacher my name is Paul,
I like to kill wild animals.
I use their skin to make my clothes,
To keep me nice and warm

My name is Bill I am the manager,
I try to protect my animals,
To keep them alive,
But the poachers try to kill them.

Adam Holley (12)
Pontarddulais Comprehensive School

ALL I WANT IS LOVE

I am feeling hate inside
when all I want is love.
I just want to run and hide
and fly away above.
Some days I just sit and cry
and want to be alone.
Sometimes I would like to die
and days I sit and moan.
By then I think - *silly me!*
Why do I feel so blue?
The birds are high up in the trees
singing so sweetly, they do.
Children playing in the street
as happy as can be.
Radios playing, happy beats
then I just start to see
that life is not that bad after all.
I have a lot of love . . .
both from my mum and from dad
I thank the Lord above.

Gemma Glenister (13)
Pontarddulais Comprehensive School

HOPE

As I sit on a hill, with the wind through my hair,
I wonder why are we here?

I look at the blooming trees and the shimmering sky
And I wonder, I wonder why?

As I stare at the sea with its mysterious hue
A tiny blue tear falls from my eye
And I wonder, I wonder why?

I gaze all around, but there's no one in sight
I'm tiring now and I give a big sigh
I still wonder, I wonder why?

Then I notice the sunset glowing up high
All the pretty colours dancing in the sky
As I peer towards the colour blaze
I look for a new tomorrow
Tomorrow's *hope!*

Catrin Brauner (11)
Pontarddulais Comprehensive School

THE SOLAR SYSTEM

Mercury's hot and fuzzy
Venus is soft and fluffy
Earth is cool and breezy
Mars is warm and greasy

Jupiter's just a bing
Saturn's with a ring
Uranus will not sing
Neptune was a king

The galaxies full of planets
Stars and suns too
Our moon is cold and icy
But so is Pluto, too

The big hole is where it all began
And then there was the big bang
The stars started shining
And then there was me.

Maryanne Temblett (12)
Pontarddulais Comprehensive School

SCHOOL

School is hard, school is tough,
Some might say you don't get enough!
I'd do without school any day,
Any century, any way,
Writing, working, it's all so hard,
I think school is *bad! bad! bad!*
School should be banned for a year or two,
Teachers don't teach you, they just torture you!
Monday, Tuesday, Wednesday, Thursday,
We may as well have it Saturday and Sunday!
Two days' rest! That's all we have,
Now that is what I call sad!

Mr Arnold, Mrs Garner, Mrs Richards and nurse too,
She'll understand what I need her to do,
'Nurse, nurse, please come over here, my belly's hurting,
                                    I've an aching head.'
'Oh dear, Holly dear, you'd better leg it back to bed.'

Holly Vipond (11)
Pontarddulais Comprehensive School

GRAMPA
(In loving memory of my grandfather)

I never knew I could hurt so much,
I guess I was so wrong,
My world has been turned upside down
Since you've been gone.
I've not only lost my grandfather,
I've lost my very best friend,
It was a crime that aged 59,
Your life had to come to an end.
The only question I can ask is, why?
Why you had to go,
But no one can answer me,
I guess I'll never know.
We looked towards the future,
You said you'd always be near,
Who would have thought at that time
You wouldn't even be here.
I hope you are watching over me,
Wherever you are now,
Rest in peace and slumber well,
Until we meet again someday, somehow.

Lauren Evans (14)
Pontarddulais Comprehensive School

ANIMALS OF THE FOREST

The birds are singing on the trees
Listening to the honey bees
Now take a look at the romping deer
They live without any fear.

Look at the rabbit making a burrow
Here comes the squirrel down the path that's narrow
Can you hear the woodpeckers pecking on the trees?
Can you hear the baby birds shouting for their teas?

Here comes the mother bird with the babies' food
But one of the baby birds was in a bad mood
He's really not feeling too happy
The food she got is far too scrappy.

The outside is full of pictures
The birds, bees, trees but not hamsters
They're at home warm in their cages
Since they were in fields it's been ages.

Charlene Davies (11)
Pontarddulais Comprehensive School

MY RABBIT

He is insane as he leaps and skips around my garden.
Trying, but not succeeding,
To jump over his run.
As he tries to dig up the garden,
My father goes furious,
As the sight of bare patches.
On the freshly cut grass,
Stand out.

When the hose pipe is out,
He runs away,
Dodging and trying to avoid.
When we are not watching,
He will eat the heads off the flowers,
He's a good weed disposer,
His brown fur gleams in the sun.
His whiskers twitch.
His name becomes clear, he's *Bobby Brown.*

Amy Davies (12)
Pontarddulais Comprehensive School

SCHOOL

As I get up on a Monday morning,
I dread to think that I have to go back to school,
Getting up at half-past seven is a horror,
But the fact I'm a year 8 in comp is cool.

As we get into school we have our registration,
and Sir asks for some cooperation,
When lunchtime comes,
I show a sigh of relief,
But I hate the thought of the afternoon.

As last lesson comes everybody is hot and bothered,
And everyone can't wait, can't wait to get home,
But it seems like last lesson lasts for hours,
As I get onto the bus I think of home,
When I get home I have a nice sleep,
And when I wake up I think about school
And I start to weep! Weep! Weep!

Ashley Lewis (12)
Pontarddulais Comprehensive School

TIMES OF YEAR

Spring: the time for a new year has come,
Everything is starting to grow,
Little birds sing high in trees above,
Squirrels scamper below,
Butterflies hatch from their cocoons,
All in the time of three months.

Summer: the time for summer has come,
The sun is like an orange hot cross bun,
The flowers are red, pink and green,
In summer rain can't be seen.

Autumn: the time that the sun goes away,
I wish summer could stay.
The green leaves have turned brown,
As they fall far down.

Winter: the time gardens are covered in snow,
When is the snow going to go?
Endless days of calm and cold,
Not much signs of the summer heat,
I can't wait for Christmas so I can have lots to eat.

Stuart Mindt (11)
Pontarddulais Comprehensive School

DREAMING

Sometimes I dream weird things
Like last night
I dreamt I had wings.

Sometimes I dream scary things
Like vampires and witches
And the ghost of dead kings.

Sometimes I dream amazing, eye-catching things
Like winning the Lottery
And buying loads of dazzling rings.

Sometimes I dream cool things
Like parties and discos
Absolutely amazing things.

Sometimes I dream impossible things
Like wearing the crown
And marrying the king.

Kirsty Wilson (12)
Pontarddulais Comprehensive School

MY PUPPY

I have a puppy,
He is black and white,
He has big, black eyes
And a big, black snout.

He runs to the yard
Like a maniac,
Trying to get out
And jumping about.

At bedtime every night,
He sleeps so soundly,
Dreaming about bones
And catching those stones.

Sara Gwynne (12)
Pontarddulais Comprehensive School

FOOTBALL MAD

My brother is a nutter
He loves the football games
He plays ball every Sunday
He plays home and away

He played football last Sunday
And he scored a hat-trick
My dad gave him a fiver
And he bought me a Twix

But later in the ball game
He scored once again - yeah!
But not for his side, oh no!
He scored against Joe James.

Leanne John (12)
Pontarddulais Comprehensive School

MY BROTHER

My brother is football mad
To me this is quite sad.
He also likes cricket too
But never gets a run or two.

My brother is rugby mad
My father thinks it's not half bad.
He thinks that I'm quite a swot
Which doesn't say an awful lot.

Tennis is his best sport,
Especially when he's on the court.
Golf is not what he does like
He prefers to climb upon his bike.

Laura Williams (12)
Pontarddulais Comprehensive School

MY DOG

I love my dog Sasha, she's very sweet.
She barks at me if I don't give her a treat.

I love my dog Sasha, I take her for lots of walks,
She eats all my grapes and just leaves me the stalks.

I love my dog Sasha, she likes to play ball,
She runs to get it so fast she headbutts the wall.

I love my dog Sasha, she's very cute.
My dad didn't think so when she ruined his best suit.

I love my dog Sasha even though she chews my shoe.
But I know that really she loves me too
But even though I am glad she's mine.

Cheryl Davies (12)
Pontarddulais Comprehensive School

STAR WARS

I like it because it's full of action,
People brave and true.
Lightsabres clashing,
Blasters flashing,
Anything like that will do.
There's Darth Maul, Obi Wan,
And Qui Gon Jinn too.
There's also R2-D2 who
helps crack codes, open doors, that's what's cool.

My favourite character is Darth Maul,
his face looks so cool, I also like his double lightsabre
that's also called a sith tool.
His sith infultrator is so huge you could fit a house
in it for refuge.
In the end the goodies win and the Empire is as good
as in the bin, so why not come along and see the best film in all eternity.

Nathan Greenwood (11)
Pontarddulais Comprehensive School

MY FAVOURITE GOLFER

To play like him,
You have got to be good
But at the moment
I don't think anyone could.

He hits the ball
Like a bullet from a gun
But when the ball hits the green
It seems to have spun.

He is ranked number one
He is the very best
He has beaten all the good ones
And topped off all the rest.

My favourite golfer is Tiger Woods
I thought you would have guessed
But you have got to admit it
He really is the best.

James Frazer (12)
Pontarddulais Comprehensive School

IN THE TWINKLE OF AN EYE

It has passed the hour on Saint Guy's tower
where the devil stays to make his power.

The devil's power remains in himself
for I have now met a powerful elf.

Be quiet, be still, the small elf was told
for this grey tower is old and cold.

I walk in the tower and smell a bad smell
for the devil can see me and casts a spell.

But the powerful elf is there at hand
to turn the bad spell to a grain of sand.

The devil is wild and curses the elf
but the evil is turned upon himself.

As we see him shrivel and slowly die
we see a small twinkle in the elf's eye.

Andrew Quinn (13)
Pontarddulais Comprehensive School

THE NIGHT

The moon shone upon the sky,
The stars twinkled in the distance.
The tree's finger nails scratched,
In the cold, frosty midnight air.
The town's buildings froze like statues,
Owls tooted in the gloomy darkness,
The eerie feeling of walking alone
Was startling.
The old, shadowy, conquered castle stood crooked
In the palpable darkness.
The city's churches and chapels' bells rang
With a tingle on each bell.
The biting weather was howling.
Nightclubs were raving with loud pumping music.
I could barely see the time by my watch,
I quietly headed on home.

Kelly Leanne Hire (11)
Pontarddulais Comprehensive School

THE CRIMINAL

Look at that car, so easy to drive
Just like that apartment you burglarised
You started to run but didn't get far
Because under your arm was a VCR

That's it now you've had it my friend
It's the end of the line, you've come to an end
You're going down, prison for life
For robbery, theft and possession of a knife

Your life has been weak, poor so far
Your family has nothing, you've dropped your VCR
I know what I'll do, I'll drive away in my car
I don't think they'll find me in Australia

Life is now good, but I'm still trying to avoid
Coppers, pigs, people think I'm paranoid
I'll just hide out here, this plan will never fail
But you never know tomorrow I could be in jail.

Dale Thomas (14)
Pontarddulais Comprehensive School

MY DOG

I have a fluffy dog,
She likes to play football,
But when I'm playing by myself,
She has to come and play.

My dog likes her choc drops,
She even has to beg.

When we take her out for walks,
It's as if she's taking me for walks.

My dog's name is Trixe, she is very nifty,
When we are having cheese
She makes a little whimper.

There's nothing more I can say,
Only that she is my dog,
And I'd never harm her.

David Taylor (12)
Pontarddulais Comprehensive School

THE BIG FILM

So this is the big day
At last it's arrived.
It's going to be big
The biggest one of all.

I've waited for so long
But now it's at an end.
I will see it tonight
But then it will be over.

But I will not worry
I will enjoy it all.
Soon will be the moment
When the film will begin.

The film will be great
The greatest of them all.
Every moment funny
The comedy of the year.

First we go to the shop
Popcorn, sweets, pop as well.
I love all sugar stuff
When watching a big film.

So here it all begins
We all take our seats.
Waiting for the big film
To amaze all of us.

And boy, does it wow us all!
The jokes, the storyline.
It is all brilliant
Right down to the ending.

Definitely worth the wait
The greatest film ever!

Thomas Reid (13)
Pontarddulais Comprehensive School

FOOD FUN

I wonder if I would be good
Made completely out of food.
Just thinking about that for me
Is my wildest fantasy.

My hair could be strawberry lace
And my eyes could be made out of grapes.
My skin would be puff pastry
And my nose would be made out of cheese.

My T-shirt would be made of chocolate
As white as white could be.
My skirt would be made of chocolate bars
Full of caramel and crème.

My shoes would be made of pick 'n' mix
That would be really fun
Eating my shoes as I walked
And my socks would be bubblegum!

What a wonderful, wonderful thought
Although it may never come true.
But a dream is forever a dream
If it comes from me or you!

Louise Lisk (11)
Pontarddulais Comprehensive School

THE SEA STORM

The waves start to roar
Seagulls no longer soar.
Fish begin to fly
The world's no longer dry.

Sudden lightning flash
Crewman creates a slash.
Snapping noise behind,
Falling mast! Please be kind.

The rain stings my face
The storm quickens its pace.
Our boat starts to tip
Get in or take a dip.

Air will soon be thin
Motors start burning.
Must make hole in keel
To get there I must kneel.

Water'll put out flames
Crewmen call out wife's names.
Cups and plates go smash
My face received a bash.

Beacon is sent out
The First Mate gets knocked out.
Rock hits starboard side
When will this storm subside?

Tempest fury wanes
No more shattered panes.
Wind no longer howls
Our boat's stopped rocking now.
Storm has now gone by . . .
Not a cloud in the sky!

Matthew Fuge (13)
Pontarddulais Comprehensive School

BUGS

Have you ever wondered
What lives in the world below?
Tiny creeping insects
Hiding places, we don't know!

Put yourself in their shoes
Even though they don't have them!
Bugs - all shapes and sizes
Smaller than the smallest gem.

Creep among the long grass
The tops too high to see.
Bugs of many colours
Flying bugs, like wasps and bees.

Many bugs to look at
Fast bugs, slow bugs, running around
Moving so carefully
Not making a single sound.

So I end my poem
With so much more to say.
Next time you're in your backyard
Remember, bugs are here to stay!

Dario Fisher (13)
Pontarddulais Comprehensive School

I HAD A DREAM

I have had a dream
To live with lions in peace
In the big jungle

Their big padded paws
Are very soft and squishy
But their claws are sharp

They would not hurt me
You see I grew up with them
So I am a friend

With their razor teeth
They can cut through meat with ease
They use their claws too

When I was quite young
They used to feed me on milk
It was delicious

When I was older
They fed me the meat they ate
It was very nice

At night it was cold
So I snuggled in their manes
They were warm and soft

In the big jungle
I feel safe with the vast pack
They would protect me

There would be fighting
But there would not be a lot
They are quite peaceful

Yes, I had a dream
I only wish it was true . . .
But it might happen!

James Freeman (13)
Pontarddulais Comprehensive School

I'VE GOT A BABY BROTHER

I've got a baby brother,
You've heard of him before.
But now he's become a part of me,
And his food's become part of the floor.

I've got a baby brother,
He's lovely and sweet with soft brown eyes.
But underneath that cute little face,
Lies the devil in disguise.

I've got a baby brother,
Who is rather small.
But he can still get into trouble,
Like scribble over the walls.

I've got a baby brother,
Who could play with his toys all day.
But when he starts to get hungry,
Don't get in his way.

I've got a baby brother,
And now he's here to stay.
But if I had a choice to make,
I could never give him away.

Kirsty Evans (13)
Pontarddulais Comprehensive School

RUGBY

The World Cup is coming to Wales,
Over the hills and across the dales.
The Welsh Dragon is flying high,
Above the Welsh Stadium and in the sky.

South Africa, Scotland and France,
New Zealand doing their Haka dance,
Wales with their hopes running high,
Passing, running, scoring a try.

First time it's been held here,
Never again for about twenty years,
We have to overcome our weaknesses and fears,
If we win, there will be lots of tears.

Christian Davies (12)
Pontarddulais Comprehensive School

JASPER THE BEAVER

Jasper, Jasper I'm so upset that he's gone
When I look at you I think of his silly ways
He made me laugh until I burst.

He used to play his flute to me while I slept.
I liked it very much.

His birthday is on the 20th October
20 is my favourite number
I feel so empty without your love.

Jasper, Jasper, you're all I've got
Jasper, please help me I am all alone
And I want to go home to Liverpool.

Zoe Davison (12)
Pontarddulais Comprehensive School

STRANDED

I'm all alone,
In this queer existence,
Of misty surroundings.
I'm trapped, trapped in the forest,
In this damp, dark whereabouts.

Every day I watch and I listen,
Watch the sun, rise and set,
Listen to the birds singing and chirping.
Alas, it has alarmingly different atmospheres.
At one moment it is happy with a meagre breeze
and wildlife freely running.
At other moments it is dark and gloomy, with heavy winds.

Please help me, I feel dirty and hot.
My only friends are the animals.
I'm stranded in this forever lasting world of loneliness.

Nicola Davidson (12)
Pontarddulais Comprehensive School

THE WIZARD

A puff of smoke, an eerie darkness,
A wave of his wand, all eyes upon him,
Drums were beating a mysterious beat,
Like millions and millions of tiny feet,
Rabbits in hats, fairies above,
Suspicion in minds, what's happening next?
Glittering lights, eyes feeling dazzled,
Crowds are amazed, cheer and gasp at the sights,
A blink of an eye, the wizard is gone,
Where did he go? No one will know.

Nicholas Howells (12)
Pontarddulais Comprehensive School

ANTICIPATION

Coloured wrappers in different shapes and sizes,
Wonder what they could be?
Waiting, waiting, waiting,
Don't put me through this agony.
Can't I just open one, or I'm
Going to explode with frustration.
I didn't know it would be such hard work,
This wait and anticipation.

Catherine Edwards (12)
Pontarddulais Comprehensive School

THE CHURCH

There was a weird-looking, battered-down church,
The bats glided around the old church,
The inky-black sky froze while the
Ferocious rats ran up and down the old church.
The tree tops scratched the weak, brown window,
Every time the clock chimes 12am
You can hear a wicked laugh.

Charlotte Thomas (11)
Pontarddulais Comprehensive School

MERLIN AND HIM!

High in a tower, inside a lofty castle,
Stood an old wizard, opening a parcel.
In a big puff of smoke a man appeared,
Wearing a cloak and a white, fluffy beard.
His hat cast a shadow, his eyes dark grey and grim,
Yet Merlin was sure, he knew it was him!

Carrie Gower (11)
Pontarddulais Comprehensive School

THE FIREWORKS DISPLAY

A shower of sparks, an explosion of flames,
Glittering fireworks light up the dark sky.
Jumping Jacks silver, with golden Catherine wheels,
All the colours are pleasing to the eye.

A blitzkrieg of rockets, an explosive noise,
The huge crowds cheer with delight and fear,
The rockets soared at an incredible pace,
They hurtled down to Earth and disappeared.

The crowd was silent, a sadness was felt,
The beautiful rockets had fallen, kaput!
The crowd turned away, the finale was over,
But many applauded the magnificent show.

Christopher Day (12)
Pontarddulais Comprehensive School

MAGICAL MISTAKE

'Abracadabra!' the great Houdini cried,
'Hocus-pocus, puffs of smoke on the side,
Audience, will you watch me disappear?
With a boom and a bang, I'm out of here.
Just one word, and I'm a flash in the pan,'
Cried he, the magical mystery man.
But dearie me, the spell went wrong you see,
Not one, not two, not even twenty-three.
People vanished, all there were banished
And left poor Houdini to stand alone,
Turn green and then fall with a strangled groan.
The great magician, perhaps for all time,
Went straight to jail for an accidental crime!

Catrin Lloyd (11)
Pontarddulais Comprehensive School

A GOOD FRIEND

What is a good friend?

A good friend is someone you can trust,
Someone who will always be there,
Someone who will not let your friendship rust.
A good friend will always be there,
someone who will listen, someone who will care.
You can tell a good friend what's on your mind
and they'll always be understanding and kind.
A good friend will help you out whatever you mention,
and they'll always give you respect and attention.
You can have a good laugh with a true friend,
and if you need something, they'll always give you a lend.
A good friend is someone you can go to places with,
Someone who will take and someone who will give.
Everyone needs someone to rely on,
Who will always be there, someone who will never be gone.

Helene Rodde (14)
Pontarddulais Comprehensive School

SPACE

Have you ever wondered about the mysteries of space?
There might be something living in that starry secret place.
Have you ever wondered how many planets would be there?
Some might be crowded some might be bare.
Have you ever wondered how many stars are in the sky?
Some are really low, some are really high.
But all these questions are going through my mind
When the answers we shall never find!

Sarah Ann Tribe (11)
Pontarddulais Comprehensive School

THE SEA OF SILENCE

The stars shimmering in the sky
so very very high.
Sparkling over the sea,
as dolphins pass by.
Jumping in the light
and crashing on the waves.
Destination unknown.

Whales singing and the sound
of peaceful bells ringing.
The moon shining so brightly,
like a power ball of light.
The sound of almighty waves
crashing wildly onto the rocks.

Suddenly . . . There's silence!

Hannah Rödde (12)
Pontarddulais Comprehensive School

FRANCE V WALES

As the boys from Wales came running out
the crowd went mental without a doubt.
As soon as the ref blows the whistle
the ball flies by like a missile.

Wales gain possession - run down the wing
despite the tackles, he's still running.
The ref blows up, a tackle too high
Neil takes the penalty in the sky.

He's done it, he's made it - no more tales
It's congrats to Neil and well done Wales.

Robert Heycock (13)
Pontarddulais Comprehensive School

WHY I DANCE

Ballet is as if you're flying, skipping, twirling, leaping and diving.
Ballet is as graceful as a swan. I will be on blocks soon, hopefully.

Modern is more acrobatic shoulder stand, side and back falls
and more.
Slipping, sliding, skidding and *splits.*
Splits the one word that I hate, yeah I know I can do them,
But you get used to it when you go dancing every night.

Tap the noisiest of them all. It is like a hundred elephants.
Stamp, stamp, stamp, stamp.
Tap dancing is in nearly all the West End shows.
Dancing is hard work but it is all worth it when you hear the roar
Of crowd and your heart starts pounding.

That's why I dance.

Natalie Sabido (12)
Pontarddulais Comprehensive School

THE PARTY

On my birthday there will be fun and laughter.
I've been excited all day long,
Just sitting there waiting for the night,
Waiting for the moment when will that party come.
There will be dancing, food and loads, loads more,
So come along and join the fun.
The fun of the party it will go on all night,
Just out there dancing, singing and jumping about.
Everybody's having fun.
So come and join the party,
The party with all of the fun.

Kirsty Roberts (11)
Pontarddulais Comprehensive School

MONEY

Money, money, I'm short of money,
I need to earn some quick,
'Dad, Dad' 'Yes honey'
'Can I have my pocket money?'
'No love not until next week.'
'But Dad you know I'm going shopping,
I'll buy you something sleek.'
'In that case I'll think about it.'
'Oh yippee how much do you reckon?'
'Well right now I'm driving to Brecon.'
I wish I had my own car,
I could drive really far.
'Thanks Dad, fifty pounds
I'll pay you back, each day a pound.'

Emma Black (12)
Pontarddulais Comprehensive School

MY DOG

My dog is white with
Brown patches on her
Her name is Siân, she's gorgeous.
I've had her since she was tiny
She used to rip things apart in the house
My mother went insane with the dog
And ever since the dog has been outside
In the kennel. When I went on holiday
We came back and she was howling
All the time. We went up to see her
And she had pups, they were all
Just sitting there yelping.

Stacey Andrews (12)
Pontarddulais Comprehensive School

HALLOWE'EN

On the 31st of October it's Hallowe'en,
And in the night the dead are supposed to be seen.
Witches and mummies, their congregation too,
We dress up as monsters oh yes we do.

Cobwebs and spiders crawl into people's beds,
To make people's eyes pop out of their heads.

Ghosts and ghouls haunt you in the night,
And when you wake up they give you a fright.

Witches fly past your window in the moonlight,
And if you see it it's a wonderful sight.

People that believe will linger about for hours on end,
Waiting for a ghost to turn around the bend.

Rhys Francis (12)
Pontarddulais Comprehensive School

GOOFY THE DOG!

I love my cuddly toys,
They're as soft as fur,
As cute as a dog,
And most of all I love them.
My favourite is Goofy the dog,
I've had him for twelve years,
Since I was born it was passed on,
And he has very long white ears.
Sometimes I wish they could talk,
Because they're as motionless as statues,
Mind you, I'll always try, when I cry,
To hold him forever and let memories pass by.

Rachel Berry (13)
Pontarddulais Comprehensive School

AUTUMN TO WINTER

Snow covers the hills,
A chill in the air blows coldly across my face,
Autumn has gone and winter is here,
Once rich golden browns, now blacks and greys.

A robin hops across the snow-covered grass,
A squirrel scuttles up a tree, to its warm winter home.
The cold winter moon shines across the icy pond.
A bird hovers above the shiny pond,
Wondering where the water's gone.

Old trees stand tall, all their leaves gone.
Their branches sticking out like spikes.
Skaters on the ice, skate elegantly round and round.
The robin picks up some twigs,
And flies back to his nest in his new home.

Alexandra Hawken (13)
Pontarddulais Comprehensive School

FLOWERS

F uschias, wonderful smells and strange shapes.
L ovely colours to occupy your gaze.
O pen in day, closed at night.
W illowing when they are dead.
E mpty plantpots in autumn and winter.
R ain droplets to magnify the pink petals.
S oon the lovely colours will be gone,
   but the picture will stay in my mind.

Bethan Turner (12)
Pontarddulais Comprehensive School

SCHOOL TIME!

School time is sometimes fun
we go to lessons, but we mustn't run.
We work really hard, we try our best.
When the time comes, we have a test.

Dinner time comes, we all line up.
We push and shove to get our grub.
After lunch we go for a walk
around the school and have a talk.

Registration is next, they call our names
then we're off, our next lesson is games.
The end of the day is here, the buzzer goes.
We all rush off to catch our bus!

Kelly Franks (11)
Pontarddulais Comprehensive School

NATURE

The fox crept through the whispering woods,
Every step was soft and quiet.

The birds sat on the thin long branches,
Tweeting away merrily.

The snake slithered through the crispy leaves,
That lay like dead mice.

The squirrel appeared from behind a tree,
Looking for its food,
Taking a glimpse now and then,
To make sure that there were no predators lurking in the shadows.

Michelle Planck (11)
Pontarddulais Comprehensive School

THE FUTURE

Who knows what the future will bring?
A change of address? A wedding ring?
Or a place in Uni with a degree?
A bright future in a dynamic company?

Virtual Reality would develop fast,
Hard labour would be in the past,
Computers would control everything!
Mechanical dogs would fetch and bring.

People would be able to live on Mars
With hovermobiles and flying cars!
Fly through space just for fun
Visit the stars but not the sun.
Motion pictures would be 3D
But I don't think the future's for me!

James Beynon (13)
Pontarddulais Comprehensive School

THE CREEPY STATION

There was a train station
Which was old and very creepy,
The station was called Park Lane Central,
It has not been used for nine years.
The station is dark, gloomy and misty
And stinks of drains.
Most of the station was made of wood and had rotted away,
But the bits that were made of stone had been untouched.
The sun never shines on the station
Because of the trees,
So the station remains cold and damp.

Christopher Gardner (11)
Pontarddulais Comprehensive School

WHAT ARE CITIES LIKE?

People awakened from their dreams
By the shining sun,
Glinting and reflecting off glass,
Bringing on the day.

Traffic racing down busy roads,
Horns and tyres squeal,
Rushing people away to work,
Hurry, don't be late.

Hurry, hurry, no time to waste
Use the cash machine;
All bargains waiting to be found,
Look what I have bought.

Quick, time to leave, shops are closing,
Try to beat the jams;
I'm starving, I'm ready for tea,
When will I get home.

Lights shining into the night sky,
Does the city sleep?
People work and people party,
Come on, let's have fun.

People awakened from their dreams,
By the shining sun;
Glinting and reflecting off glass,
Bringing on the day.

Laura Buckingham (11)
Pontarddulais Comprehensive School

RUGBY WORLD CUP 1999

The Millennium Stadium is the new destination
Its magnificent structure is a complete revelation
The large roof can easily be removed
So come rain or shine the pitch can be used.

The opening ceremony of the World Cup Rugby
Was entertaining and wonderful to see
The music and Welsh singers amazed the crowd
Who applauded and cheered ever so loud.

Dancers performed with sweet children singing
The people joined in with all voices ringing
A large red dragon was built on the field
And at the roar of the fire the people cheered.

Excited fans to Cardiff did travel
To see how the rugby game would unravel
Wales and Argentina in the opening game
Competing to seek their moment of fame.

As the first whistle blew, the match began
And all the players tackled and ran
Tension mounted as the Argentineans scored
But as Wales took the lead the crowd all roared.

The Welsh team did us proud and we will never forget
Will the game in this stadium be the best yet?
Whatever the outcome of our home side
We will support the Welsh team with pride.

Ruth McCarry (14)
Pontarddulais Comprehensive School

MY GRAN

I love my gran
    always happy
    never sad
    never grumpy
    never mad

As gentle and as tender as a newborn
puppy. She's always there when I
need her. No matter what she's doing
always courteous, always daring.

    Strong and sturdy like a rock
    caring, sharing everything
    she's got.
    I love my gran.

Nicola Cox (13)
Pontarddulais Comprehensive School

OVERBOARD

Out tonight I was holding tight,
Men were jumping overboard.
Will I be next?
I wish you were here to save me.

Children holding on for their dear lives.
Will I be next?
I wish you were here to save me!

Out tonight I was holding tight,
Ladies on their knees praying, praying to the Lord,
Will I be next?
I wish, I wish you were here to save me.

Claire Mainwaring (12)
Pontarddulais Comprehensive School

PIE FEVER

I must go home for my tea, for the lovely look of a pie,
For I'm a pie lover and I will tell you why,
A mince pie, a chicken pie, even a pie filled with curry,
Whatever size or shape it is, I'll eat it in a hurry.

I must go home for my tea again,
Because my tummy is starting to rumble,
It's rude, a rude call that upsets everyone.
What I need is a giant pie to pass and touch my lips,
Like a steak pie with brown sauce on it and a massive pile of chips.

I've just got home for my tea again, but I had a frightening surprise,
My mum made a horrible salad, instead of the usual pies.
When I said I did not want to eat it, Mum calls me a disgrace,
So I did eat the salad, but I gave some to the dog,
My mother said, 'Where's it gone?' and I said, 'I ate it all.'

Kevin Davies (13)
Pontarddulais Comprehensive School

THE BARN

The creaking doors would open and close,
All I could see was dark figures in the dark barn.
Hooting owls were everywhere,
Why won't the barn disappear . . .
It was a mystery.
The barn across the road stood out like a 3D picture,
But this is more repulsive and ghastly.
It was *there*.

Johnathan Davies (12)
Pontarddulais Comprehensive School

WHY ME, WHY?

I knew I was different, I have been all my life,
My parents rejected me when I was small.
I was separated, put aside, ignored all the time,
Why me, why?

I started schools again and again,
None were right for me.
It wasn't the schools it was the people,
Why me, why?

I was born that way; I'm embarrassed by it,
It's not my fault or anyone else's.
I look in the mirror, what I see I hate.
Why me, why?

I can't go outside *they* will get me,
Inside *they* get me too.
They always shout abuse in terror,
Why me, why?

One day I saw it on the news,
How easy it looked to me.
The itchy rope around my neck,
Suddenly my troubles were over.
Why me, why?

Rachel Buckley (13)
Pontarddulais Comprehensive School

THE DRAGGING FEET

Dragging down the grey dull path, a gloomy miserable day,
The cold tingled and whistled,
Wolves howled and cats miaowed.

The winter frost drilling into her tough strong nature,
Her parents shrieking in the background,
No other thought ran through their tiny
Little midget-size brains, except competing words,
And the only thing they had in common
Was the same daughter.
Sixteen year old, lonely, sad daughter.
Mean. Selfish. Slimy. Miserly. Stingy.
Despicable, so-called 'parents'.
Mean.
Plain and simple, mean.

She returned to a world of slow-paced steps,
But why? She had a life too!
Those ignorant parents had actually,
Finally stopped arguing!
She stood there gaping, amazed at the
Palpable silence.
Silence . . .
Silence . . .
Silence . . .

Kirsty Joseph (13)
Pontarddulais Comprehensive School

GAZING OUT TO SEA

A splash of a wave,
The cry of a seagull,
The smell of seaweed,
The fish swim fast,
In the sea.

Lightning strikes,
The crashing thunder,
Darkness surrounds us,
The moon comes out,
In the sky.

The silence is peaceful,
The ground feels cold,
On the land.

Kayleigh James (12)
Pontarddulais Comprehensive School

FRIGHTENED

A creepy noise a weird spooky night
In the darkness I saw something bright.
When I turned around I had a tear
My stomach was full of churning fear.

Before my eyes stood a quivering shadow.
With swirling clothes and eyes so shallow.
I stood there stunned with my eyes shut tight.

I opened my left eye and went to run.
I turned around and saw my mum.
Though I realised it was a horrid dream.
I still sat up and started to scream.

Danielle Rees (12)
Pontarddulais Comprehensive School

THE JAGUAR CAR

At last we're off - zooming down the road
In our new Jaguar car.
Radio blaring and tyres burning
Speeding through the traffic lights.

Taking the corner at 90 miles per hour
Skidding past the school at night.
Radio blaring and tyres burning
Speeding through the traffic lights.

Sirens are heard and police lights flash
Can't make the bend - head-on crash.
Radio blaring and tyres burning
Speeding through the traffic lights.

Paul Elliott (13)
Pontarddulais Comprehensive School

WITCHES

The witches come out on a starry night
A night filled with horror, a night filled with death.
Piercing screams could be heard from the town
Showing that magic was forever around.

Faces so ugly they torture your eyes
Cauldrons bubbling with poisons and badness
Thinking of death and torture to humans.

Messengers of the Devil - stalkers of the night
Their little black cats with little green eyes
Grin because they know the evil secret
Between you and me . . .
You and me . . . You and me!

Ayat Tahir (12)
Pontarddulais Comprehensive School

READING

Everyone's got a hobby, everyone's got a passion,
For some like me it's reading,
Taking part in murder plots.

Imagine a library, full of books,
Comfy chairs and a photocopier,
But the highlight of the library,
Is the book-covered shelves,
What if that was your favourite place?

The librarian with her lovely smile,
Her ironed dress and her shiny shoes,
Helping you choose your books,
What if that was your favourite person?

Sitting down reading a thick book,
The cover warm to the touch,
Your library card ready for action,
The book an exciting novel,
What if that was your ideal day?

If it is then good for you,
Reading has many advantages,
Your grammar and writing gets better,
What if English was your favourite lesson?

Charlene Smith (13)
Pontarddulais Comprehensive School

DINOSAURS!

Dinosaurs are musty things
They have long tails and scaly skin.
There's T-rex, triceratops and raptors too.
They cannot be found in a zoo.
I would like to go back and see them
but really I would love to be one.
Tyrannosaurus rules as king
a velociraotor jumps like a spring.
But until then I'll go to the museum
if I really want to see them.

Our pets are really mild
but dinosaurs are really wild.
They are as tall as skyscrapers
and they conquered acres.
I would love to play with them
while other people bellow 'Run!'
I love dinosaurs every single one
I don't understand why people yell 'Run!'

I'd like to be an archaeologist
trying to find bones in the mist.
There's a dinosaur that stands above the rest
he's a tyrannosaurus rex.

David Carl Miles (12)
Pontarddulais Comprehensive School

NUTS ARE RIPE

The nuts are ripe
The flowers have gone
The ferns are brown
The apples are ready to pick
And the wind is blowing

The squirrels are harvesting
The hedgehogs are sleeping
The leaves are dying
The trees are swaying

The swallows have gone
The nights are long
The wind is blowing on
The rain has now gone.

Sarah Brown (13)
Pontarddulais Comprehensive School

NOISES IN THE DISTANCE

As the bats fly by,
And freaky ghosts sigh by,
Metal bars clanging together at night,
Rain hammering down,
Storms coming over,
Dark is closing in,
Smoke everywhere,
As if there are fires,
Door hinges squeaking,
Storms hammering down,
Ghosts hitting the door,
Darkness everywhere.

Amy Kelly (11)
Pontarddulais Comprehensive School

LIFE

Life is full of questions and answers.
The problem is to tell the difference.
Light or dark, good or bad.
The choices are clear, yet they're so hard.

Which way now, to run or fight?
Stand up and be counted, make your way.
Stand aside, shrink back and hide
The choices are clear, yet they're so hard.

To keep a friend or to be disliked!
How hard to try, what length to go?
To follow along or just say no!
The choices are clear, yet they're so hard.

Leyah Hillman (14)
Pontarddulais Comprehensive School

MY WEDDING

White dress flowing, silk pumps showing.
The bride dazzles down the aisle.
Pageboys, bridesmaids, flower girls too
My wedding dream has just come true.

The groom is waiting at the altar
With a very nervous smile.
Best man holding wedding rings,
Organ plays as choirboy sings.

At the end we have a party
Everybody laughs and dances.
The food is great, the ale flows
We all get so drunk . . . Heaven knows!

Sara Lloyd (13)
Pontarddulais Comprehensive School

FUDGE (1972 - 1999)

I love my riding hat,
I like to go out on a hack,
I put the saddle on my horse's back.
I sat on my horse's back.
I like riding in May,
My horse needed a lot of hay,
I like riding on the moor,
My horse needed a lot of straw,
My horse wasn't a pain,
She was faster than a train,
I could feel the breeze,
I could touch the trees,
With one hand on her mane,
And one hand holding the reins,
With my feet in my riding boots,
And my riding boots in the stirrups,
I felt like a bird flying through the trees,
We used to ride through streams,
And jump over beams,
I once had a dream about my horse and me
Jumping over a ten foot beam,
But now that dream won't come true,
Because now my horse has gone to a nice place above
To see all the horses and ponies that she once loved.

Laura Harvey (12)
Pontarddulais Comprehensive School

WELSH FLAG, SYMBOL OF PRIDE

W   Welsh flag I wave with pride
E   Elegant dragon at its centre
L   Lush green at the bottom
S   Snowy white on the top
H   Hail the flag of Wales

F   Freedom was the cry of Wales
L   Legendary to us all
A   Admired by all nations
G   Glad to be Welsh and live in Wales

S   Sincere to Wales
Y   You should worship it
M   Many countries admire it
B   Bold, big, bravado
O   Our minds swirl when we see it
L   Loads of people love it

O   Our symbol of pride
F   Forever it will last

P   People of the world all recognise it
R   Represents our strength
I   Indicates our power
D   Dragon of red on it
E   Everyone loves it.

Tom Williams (12)
Pontarddulais Comprehensive School

241

MY GRAMPA

I am missing you Grampa
I am missing you Grampa!
You had a heart of gold
Which was split into two.
Half for me and half for you.
Please come home . . . I miss you so.

I can feel you near me
I know you loved me lots.
I don't know why you aren't here
But I know you can't come back.
I know you are in Heaven
I know you are safe there.
Please come home . . . I miss you so.

Natalie Wassell (13)
Pontarddulais Comprehensive School

SUMMER

As the summer sun shines down,
Upon the golden sand,
As the waves come splashing in,
Children are being grand.

Not everyone is on the beach,
Some have gone into town,
To buy some new clothes today,
Because the sun is here to stay.

As the harvest moon comes out,
In the silent sky,
As the cuckoos sing their song,
In a lullaby.

Nicola Benson (11)
Pontarddulais Comprehensive School

BOOKS

Books are here, books are there,
How many types can you find?
Adventure, fiction, real life and love,
Sci-fi, comics and more.
Pick one up, it's not a bore.

Find your own style and write your own book,
Come on to a world of fantasy,
Come to a world of imagination,
Take a step to a new friend,
Or battle through the Great World War.

Hide under rocks, climb over stone,
Don't resist you could be clever,
You could be *cool!*

Martin Nelson (13)
Pontarddulais Comprehensive School

A HAUNTED HOUSE

It was a dark, gloomy night,
The rain began to fall heavy on the window,
It got louder.
It began to seep through the dark, scary basement,
Drip, drip, the clouds mixed together,
To make a funny blacky colour,
Then all of a sudden a big flash of lightning struck outside,
The night was getting scarier.
The clock struck 12 o'clock,
I could feel the ghostly touch on my hands like frozen ice.
The rain began to slow down,
A frost formed.

Leanne Andrews (11)
Pontarddulais Comprehensive School

MY FAVOURITE ANIMALS

Dolphins are cute,
Dolphins are cute,
They screech and splash,
That's why they're cute.

Crabs, they hurt,
Crabs, they hurt,
They pinch and bite,
That's why they hurt.

Sea creatures, they're silent,
Sea creatures, they're silent,
They swim not talk,
That's why they're silent.

Snakes, they slither,
Snakes, they slither,
They've got no legs,
That's why they slither.

Pigs, they're dirty,
Pigs, they're dirty,
They roll in the mud . . .
You know the rest!

Anyway, but now I've decided,
After all this I like snakes,
Hiss, hiss, hiss.

Rebecca Barton (11)
Pontarddulais Comprehensive School

MY PET

My mum's a housewife, my dad's a chef,
I love to have my father's best.
I've got a normal life, not much to do,
but when summer holidays come I have a lot to do.

I nag my parents to have my own way,
But they end up telling me to go away.
I want an elephant for a pet, because I
know elephants are some of the best.
My parents said no they don't want a mess,
but I know they will say yes.

I got my elephant and kept it as a pet,
he really did stupid things and so I took him to the vet.

I squeezed him into the waiting room,
but when I sat down a woman gave a shout
and so I had to take him out.
I had to take my elephant back, from where I had got him.

No more was he my elephant, no more was he my friend,
no more was he my pet, no more did I have to take him to the vet.

He was the best from all the rest, I do feel sad
and giving him away makes me feel even bad,
But to cheer myself, I remind myself,
Summer holidays are on the way.

Huma Pervez (13)
Pontarddulais Comprehensive School

FRIDAY AFTERNOON

Walking home from school on a Friday afternoon.
Excited for the weekend
I burst through my door,
Like a bull charging through a field
I go and get changed.
My mum shouts 'Get that room tidied.'
But I say 'Mum I want some food.'
The school meals are lovely
But now I'm very hungry
I say 'What's for tea Mum?'
She says 'A burger, chips and a bun.
And after that you can get that room tidy.'
Oh no!
I wish it wasn't Friday!

Rhian Harris (12)
Pontarddulais Comprehensive School

A SCHOOL DAY!

School has lots of subjects
Science, English, maths
Drama, art and DT,
make a fun school day for me!

When dinner time comes around
I run and line up,
I can't wait for dinner time
which I like very much!

At the end of school we all run out
to go and catch the bus
Then the buses pull away
after the mad rush!

Charlotte Button (11)
Pontarddulais Comprehensive School

CLAUDIA CAT!

Claudia is a pussycat with claws as sharp as talons.
All day long she's out in the woods climbing trees and hedges.
Then she's falling out of them.
I have seen her a couple of times stuck in a tree miaowing
Then I hear an awful *crash*
And she has fallen out of it.

Her favourite place of shelter is the bird table in the garden
I often see her sitting in it sunning her little tummy.

I reckon that she's quite odd when it comes to eating fish.
She will eat the tinned fish but seems not to like fresh fish.

But I still like her an awful lot because she's so friendly and so playful.
But now my little pussy cat and I will have to go *miaow!*

Jemma O'Brien (11)
Pontarddulais Comprehensive School

CREEPY CASTLE

It was the middle of the night,
In the middle of the winter,
I was walking in a deep, dark forest,
I was so scared.
My heart was in my throat,
Bats were watching me,
Squirrels running on the leaves,
And it's a full moon.
I gasped as I saw a huge castle,
I needed shelter,
It was really creepy.
It was like a Goosebumps episode,
But this time it was real.

Ben Matthews (12)
Pontarddulais Comprehensive School

THE CAR CRASH

As I ran towards the crash
I saw a crowd gathering
The shattered remains of the car
Lay upside down upon the road
I heard the drip, drip of petrol
And thought 'It is going to blow!'
Then I heard a person screaming.

Followed by sirens coming
The flashing lights approaching
The boys in blue nearing
The jingling of glass cracking
The firemen arrive and start cutting people free
Finally the people are out
And they are not injured.

Then suddenly the car blows
The explosion shatters windows
For half a mile around
Glass falls, alarms start to ring
The roasting heat singes my face
The crackling of fires
And the dancing of flames.

I head away from the scene
And forever more my mind
Replays that horrible scene
Until my dying day.

Rhys Turner (13)
Pontarddulais Comprehensive School

POLAR BEAR CUB

Once again a bitterly cold night falls,
A lonely feeling clouds over the Arctic,
Sending a lost Polar bear cub
Searching, wandering,
His chunky ashen paws sinking deeply into the soft snow,
The Polar bear's fear grows stronger every second.

He stops to rest by a rock,
Which shelters him from heavy falling snow,
His mother is nowhere to be seen,
The Polar bear heaves himself slowly onto his tired legs
and trudges off.

Suddenly he hits a frozen lake and slides,
The ice cracks and splits,
The cub cries for his mother,
His grip loosens and he crashes into the water.

Down, down the frightened cub sinks,
He feels as cold as an icicle and he stiffens,
Then the cub feels a tug and is lifted up out of the water
And he is dragged onto a heap of snow.

He opens his eyes and to his relief he sees his mother!
The baby bear grabs onto her warm fur,
The mother and cub make their way through the blinding snow,
To get to their cosy underground den.

Rachel Gibbon (11)
Pontarddulais Comprehensive School

HENRY'S MARVELS

We have Howarth in the backs
The Quinnels in the attack.
Charvis with the tries
Gibbs with the surprise.
Jenkins with the kick
The English with the stick.
We hear Howley sing
And Henry is our king.

We have Wyatt as our lock
And Rogers as our prop.
Wyatt in the second row
Taking every lineout throw.
Dafydd James scores a try
Graham Henry with a tear in his eye.

Mark Phillips (13)
Pontarddulais Comprehensive School

WHICH DREAM-LIT WORLD?

My eyes sealed as I drifted off,
I saw the blue-lit sky.
The breeze brushed across my
Pale, freckled face.
It lifted me higher than high,
Drifting by like a lonely cloud
Amongst the wind and breeze.
Low and lower, enclosing on the trees,
A swirl of autumn leaves,
Descending now as my eyes swirled,
And I awoke into my dream-lit world.

Emma Louise Bolt (13)
Pontarddulais Comprehensive School

THE CHILD

She walks the street with a frown on her face
Searching, looking for whom?
She stops and sits and waits for a bit,
As her heart breaks in two,
As she looks at the remains
Of what used to be,
Alone, empty, she sits,
For now the child is all alone,
Her heart and faith smashed to bits,
All she has is what you see,
Now it's her alone,
Forever, alone, she will be,
Searching, looking for home.

Nicola Hearne (13)
Pontarddulais Comprehensive School

MY GRANDMA

My grandma is a real fusspot,
She fiddles all day long.
And when she gets bored,
She would sit and stare at the wall.

She has cheeks
As red as a rose
And wrinkles down her face.

She likes to watch Eastenders
But doesn't like Star Wars.
She hates to watch Coronation Street
But doesn't mind Brookside.

Jamie Clement (11)
Pontarddulais Comprehensive School

THE TITLE IS UP TO YOU!

My worst nightmare has come true
Pain, suffering, loss of hope,
Family and friends torn apart.

NATO bombs, Kosovo again!
Targeting the enemy bases,
The noise of buildings,
Falling with a *bang* to the ground.

Refugees, trying to get away,
Fleeing to the nearest countries,
Kosovans, mainly men, being taken away,
Killed in front of their children's eyes.

People crying as they beg for help,
Asking for our nation's support,
Food, clothing, water and shelter,
All scarce during the long, cold hours.

Mother, father, sister, brother,
Holding out their hands,
As Tony Blair visits their camps,
Promising that everything will be all right.

Everyone praying,
To the Lord God above,
That he will help them,
To fight for another day.

Search deep down,
Into the chest of emotions
And find a way to include,
In your prayers tonight,
That the bombings will come to an end
And family and friends can be reunited again.

Sharon-Louise Jones (15)
Pontarddulais Comprehensive School

SILENCE

The silence engulfed the land,
The silence reined supreme,
The street and tiny gardens bathed in moonlight,
For only her to see.

A hedge, placed in a corner of a silvery garden,
The rustling loud in the silence,
A head with twinkling eyes, reflecting the moon,
A sleek russet body, a narrow cunning nose.

A pattering of practised steps and she is there,
Strong, yet weak in this tumultuous world,
Tiny dappling paw prints printing in a flower bed,
She waits, there is a movement.

With a snap of her jaws she has her prize
And curls, curls her body up to savour the delicacy,
Her bushy tail curled around thin legs,
She sighs sadly, as if she is fed up with life.

A man comes out, disrupting her silence,
As quick as a flash she whips her body,
Away from me, to a safe place, her place.

As the purr of the car drives away,
I am left with silence, once her silence,
She, with glistening intelligent eyes,
Left with the cool moonlight bathing the street.

I look to the whispering sky, full of secrets,
At the billowing clouds, the twinkling stars,
And I creak towards the noise,
My noise.

Coralie Mouncher (13)
Pontarddulais Comprehensive School

WHO IS HE?

Sitting there as quiet as can be
Scared of the big white beard dangling
off his face, and the scary eyebrows
thick, bushy and grey. He's
staring at me weirdly
What's he staring at?

He's got his hands around me,
What's he going to do? Oh
Mum's taking a photo 'Smile'
she said. Now I'm trying
to get down. I'm standing firmly
on the floor.
Oh look he has a present
It's for me 'Yippee!'

Now I really love him but
what was he dressed up as?
I wonder wearily.
His coat is as red as blood
and his shoes, as black as
a blackboard,
his white beard stands out a
mile, as white as chalk can be!
But still who
is he?
Perhaps I'll find
out next year!

Briony Ruth Frayne (12)
Pontarddulais Comprehensive School

CAPTAIN PHILIP BOSWIRTH R I P

Here they stand, six hundred and four,
Here they stand in the ice-cold morn.
Not knowing whether to stay or whether to run.
They unsheathe their sabres,
Here they come to aid our European neighbour.
Not knowing whether to stay or whether to run,
The Lion coming to strike the Bear.
And came the order 'Forward Light Brigade' as he spurred on his mare,
Not knowing whether to stay or whether to run.
'Charge! Men charge! Show the world that we care,'
Onward they charged the guns of the Bear.
Not knowing whether to stay or whether to run.
They cannot be expected to do this, they are unable,
They could only carry this off if they were indomitable.
Not knowing whether to stay or whether to run.
This is mocking Death and this charge has become a maul,
The bugler had called 'Tactical Withdrawal'.
Not knowing whether to stay or whether to run.
Three quarters of the six hundred made the ultimate sacrifice,
The quarter that was left skulked back like mice.
Wishing they had not stayed, wishing they had run.
The humiliation of the British Army and Lady Britannia,
The humiliation of the French Cockerel.
They had failed dismally because of the wrong order,
They had fought because of the Russian Border.
This is the poor story of he,
Captain Philip Boswirth R I P.

Alistair Veck (13)
Pontarddulais Comprehensive School

MY LAPTOP

My laptop makes me happy
My laptop makes me sad
And when the system crashes it makes me really mad.

If I break the computer
My parents go mad
I get into lots of trouble
And that makes me really sad.

There is a CD ROM, floppy disk and lots more
Last week I did an upgrade
That went terribly wrong
I broke the hard disk
That was very wrong.

I bought a new game
It was a lovely game to play
But I dropped it on the floor
What more could I say.

When it is 6:00pm
It is time for me to go on-line
I play cards in Russia
And chess in Toulouse

I wish I could invent a system
Before I am 24
Similar to Mr Gates' 'Windows',
But I'd call mine 'Doors'.

Dylan Lewis (12)
Pontarddulais Comprehensive School

SHE IS . . .

We are like a flower blooming with
new shades each year.
If a petal plunges to the ground, we pull together
robust and refill the gap.
This is our friendship.

When I am downcast she seems to comprehend,
but when I am happy she *knows.*
Her eyes are alive dancing like stars in the dark,
bleak dead of night.

She is my companion, my partner, my friend.
Though she is not human she had very powerful
emotions that grab me sternly.
I feel what she feels.

Memories I have with her are great.
She has always been spontaneous.
She seems to have a spring in her tail
and a spark in her heart.

She is my north star shining incredibly bright,
always guiding me. She'll never reduce in this
because she is my friend. She is in my heart,
even when she's gone. I dread that day.
She will then have half my heart
and I'll have half of hers,
so that we are never apart.

Sarah Richards (13)
Pontarddulais Comprehensive School

THE SEASONS

Winter has come and the snow starts to fall,
Plants and trees don't grow very tall,
We play in the snow night and day,
Then eventually the snow melts away.
It's springtime again,
Hip, hip hooray!

Spring has come and lambs are born,
Plants and trees start to grow tall,
The leaves on the trees regain their colour,
In a couple of weeks it will be summer.
Summer is next,
I think summer is the best!

Summer is here,
Hip, hip hooray,
The sun shines brightly all through the day,
The flowers are blooming, the grass is green,
I think this summer's
The best I've seen!

Next we have autumn,
When the weather gets duller,
The leaves start to fall
And the trees change their colour,
The animals get ready to hide themselves away
And sleep through the winter till spring comes to stay!

Jaimee Davies (11)
Pontarddulais Comprehensive School

SEASONS

Spring

Spring is bright, cold and wet
People need their gloves but they forget
Going up the street soaking wet
Needing a scarf that they can't get.

Summer

Summer is the warmest one
Children playing, having fun
People using water guns, and going in their pools.

Autumn

Summer's gone and autumn's here
Getting colder by the year
Leaves are falling off the trees, changing colours as they fall

Winter

Snow is falling, freezing cold
Skiers skiing on the hills
Children playing on their sleighs
When Father Christmas gets his prey
People playing on their trays
Sliding down the icy fields
Snow is dropping off the trees
As they feel the gentle breeze.

Matthew Elvins (11)
Pontarddulais Comprehensive School

SEASONS

Spring is full of happiness
Flowers are blooming in the grass,
Leaves are green in the trees,
Squirrels run across the park,
Water's clean like a fresh spring,
Young birds chirping in the trees,
Grass is fresh.

Summer sun in the sky,
Burning on the back of my neck,
Sweat running down my face,
Ice-cream vans driving past,
Busy bees in the sky,
Going for a swim in the lake,
Dogs are panting, out of breath.

Autumn's full of crispy leaves,
Brown and crinkly,
Falling off the trees,
A man with dogs jogging past,
Hallowe'en is soon to pass,
Witches, ghost, ghouls and bats,
Watch out for those big black cats.

Winter's the time for snow,
Bonfires light up the night,
Snow falls on my head,
Fingers and toes are going dead,
Christmas is drawing near,
Christmas turkey looks so nice,
Especially with cherry brandy and ice.

Bradleigh Brooks (14)
Pontarddulais Comprehensive School

IMAGES OF THE BLITZ!

Weeping, weeping, weeping,
She sat still as a rock,
In a bloody-red frock,
As the bombs came down.

Weeping, weeping, weeping,
Her rocking chair creaked,
As she rocked back and fore,
Waiting for her love.

Weeping, weeping, weeping,
Her legs are cut,
Her arms are bruised,
And her heart is broken,
Waiting for her love.

Weeping, weeping, weeping,
A picture to her chest,
A picture of love,
The ghostly expressions,
Weeping, weeping, weeping.

Andrew Richards (12)
Sir Thomas Picton School

WAR

Bomb blasts,
Rations ahoy,
Nightly raids going off,
Tearful eyes breaking
into cries,
'Hitler!'

Charlotte Morgan (12)
Sir Thomas Picton School

WORLD WAR TWO POEM

My grandad and grandma were in the war you know,
It wasn't very nice!
All the bombs and all the guns,
It wasn't a pretty sight.

'Gather in the air raid shelters' everybody said,
As we're about to fight,
Frightened people go inside,
Hoping that their family's alright.

Feeling sorry for the people whose family's died,
Knowing they tried their best,
Angry, devastated but glad that Grandma and Grandad did survive,
Praise the Lord for all those women and men.

The war was over, how happy people were,
A couple of days in the air raid shelter wasn't very nice,
A lot of people dead, a lot of people lost,
Very happy to see our family once again.

Greetings and cuddles everywhere,
Seeing your loved ones again,
It was really nice to know
That your family was alright.

For the people whose families have died,
We're very sorry for them,
Our best wishes we do send
And our deepest sympathies as well.

Walking to our house,
Seeing the fallen-down buildings,
Hoping we'd still have a place to live,
And finding that we are lucky as we have.

That's my poem about the war,
I hope you did enjoy it.

Natalie Carol Mayhew (13)
Sir Thomas Picton School

WAR'S OVER

Come on out! It's stopped,
Towns left in one piece are at rest,
British troops are coming home from battle,
Some died, some lived,
People are now cheerful that the terror has gone.

We have victory, we have scored,
We have our freedom, but will never be the same again,
Some never came back from the gateway from hell,
But the smell of burnt flesh is still in the air,
Armed marching soldiers are no longer roaming the streets.

Buildings have broken like a house of cards,
The impassive Germans had broken from battle,
Our children are coming back from all over,
The sky is clear, the Germans we fear no more,
The sound of machine guns is no longer heard.

Many have already started to rebuild their lives,
Mothers and wives wait to see sons and husbands,
Tears are falling like leaves off a tree,
The planes that once flew over our heads are now gone,
But the sadness is still around!

Paul Evans (12)
Sir Thomas Picton School

WHY?

Why?
Why is there war
With its unnecessary evil?
Unwanted pain?

Why?
Why is there war
With its unjust suffering
And death?

Why?
Why is there war?
Bloodthirsty people
Fighting for power.

How?
How long for its end
For harmony and peace
And happiness?

How?
How long for its end.
For agreement, placidty
And mirth?

What?
What does war bring?
False hope and false glory.

What?
What does war bring?
No pleasure but pain.
Evil without gain.

Freedom!
Freedom is lacking, but
Why?

Heather Coles-Riley (12)
Sir Thomas Picton School

THE WASH TOWER

Walking down the crumbly road
Going to wash
Crowds walking round
Shaking. Scared.
Then we reach The Wash Tower,
Big brown doors opening slowly,
Squeaking loudly.
People piling through the old doors.
Then the doors bang shut!
Silence occurs,
Green smoky gas starts falling from the ceiling
Like leaves falling from an autumn tree.
Screaming, shouting,
The sound of ripping flesh
Silence.
Bodies piled up in The Wash Tower.

Laura Cornish (12)
Sir Thomas Picton School

WAR!

Smoke was everywhere,
So you couldn't see far,
But you could see enough to frighten you out of your wits.

Dusty bombs that had hit the ground that night,
Children and their parents were filled with fright.

They looked around to see a bomb, which had hit the street that night,
Factories were working quickly,
They had to make up for the time lost the night before.

Flats which people used to live in,
Were three stories high,
But now it's gone.

Blood on the floor surrounding the cold, dead bodies,
A loud noise came from a building,
It was an old lady screaming for dear life.

Bethan Phillips (12)
Sir Thomas Picton School

BRITISH BULLDOGS

Confusion and chaos,
Plus panic and pain,
Bloodthirsty with hatred,
But will anything gain?

From the destruction and death,
And the yearn to cease,
The obscene devastation,
British Bulldogs, please bring peace.

Laura Clements (12)
Sir Thomas Picton School

WAR!

I see the bodies lying there,
With loved ones next to them in
Despair.

And all the houses bombed down
To the ground,
And little children who've not yet
Been found.

The air raid siren has long been
stopped,
As the big huge bomb had long
been dropped.

Becky Gau (12)
Sir Thomas Picton School

WAR!

Dark and cold,
It was that night,
Screaming sirens fill the air.

People rushing, panicking,
Looking for a place to hide,
Away from the smoke,
The ghastly smell,
The blood of the dead.

I'm only a child,
Help me get away,
From this destructive war.

Rachel Lewis (12)
Sir Thomas Picton School

WAR!

The skies are dark and grey,
Evening time is coming near,
People rushing from here and there,
Getting ready for the unknown night ahead,
Houses closing up for the night,
Lights not able to be seen in sight.

The skies are starting to rumble,
Bellowing sounds are drawing near,
Sirens are screeching out loud,
Bombs falling here and there,
Exploding like fire balls everywhere,
The skies are now all alight and bright.

The night is long with big thuds above,
But eventually they disappear away,
We have no clue what's in stall
Outside the shelter's doors,
Soon will come the safe siren,
Carefully we will emerge.

The skies are still,
There is a smell of death in the air,
We opened the door,
There were houses all in rubble,
And bodies lying there dead.
The city will never be the same again.

Sara-Jane Jones (12)
Sir Thomas Picton School

THE WAR

As I watched in devastation
My friends and family were sundered,
Crying in a dark, shaded corner
I sat, I thought, I wondered.

I watched as buildings were destroyed
Those felons I'll never forgive,
They've done so much damage
And caused so much pain, only a few will live

With a frightened smug-faced smile
I grinned at life in empty joy,
I saw a little girl very aject
As she has now lost her childhood toy.

My stomach felt like a ball of butterflies
My heart sliced like a cake,
Dead bodies, flesh rotting, I was frightened and sick
This war was a terrible mistake.

I am stuck in the Valley of Death
Why has this happened? Why was it done?
Bombs dropped like giant footsteps
They sounded as if they weighed a ton.

The war has ended, that I know
My heart can't take any more,
How powerful and strong this fight was
The war was not a bore.

Danielle Edwards (12)
Sir Thomas Picton School

THE BULGING BOMB

As I close my eyes I feel a sensation of darkness,
It feels like nothing, apart from a deep, dark cave,
I see devastated faces scurrying through the undergrowth
Looking for what they have got left,
The night returns and all is well,
A bombing Spitfire, looking for hell.

I feel scared, miserable and destroyed.

Barry Bowen (13)
Sir Thomas Picton School

WAR

Air raid
Run from the bombs
Hide in the bomb shelter
Hope you will survive the
night, till
All-clear.

Christopher Strzelecki (12)
Sir Thomas Picton School

PEACE

Quiet,
All by myself,
Thinking, dreaming, alone.
Distant sounds of song and laughter.
Peaceful.

Helen Bowden (12)
Sir Thomas Picton School

WAR, WAR AND WAR

A look of terror in his eyes
As he lies lifeless, dead to the world,
My body shakes as my emotions spill,
I think of death, sadness and devastation.
Dirty, pointless, dark War.
His limbs abroad along the street,
Blood pouring down his blue bruised cheek,
His pain shows now,
He's not so strong,
Like when he fought
From dusk to dawn.
Dirty, pointless, dark War.
Why can't harmony light up our darkness
To cheer us up and stop us crying.
I see a screaming child, a weeping mother
As they stand over a shot-down father.
Dirty, pointless, dark War.
He fought for his country,
And died determined,
To stop our lives of all our hurting.
Dirty, pointless dark War.
Ruins his life and many others,
Dirty, pointless, dark War.
My life apart,
I look around
At what is left,
Sundered lives, cowed.
I'm scared, I'm angry
And I yearn to see the day when I escape this misery.
Dirty, pointless, dark *War!*

Annie Slater (12)
Sir Thomas Picton School

PEACE

Safety
Air raids vanished,
Everybody happy,
Everybody peaceful and calm,
Laughter.

Arrun Shaw (12)
Sir Thomas Picton School

PEACE

Peace is
Love, happiness.
Peace is found in the heart.
Peace brings golden doves with words so
Gentle.

Amanda Rayworth-Kiernan (12)
Sir Thomas Picton School

WAR

Sirens
People screaming
Houses being destroyed
The *peace* shattered by bombs flying
and *death*.

Vincent Thorne (12)
Sir Thomas Picton School

WAR

Sirens
Sound in panic
People run in alarm
The war has made chaos, no one
Can run.

Verity Halls (12)
Sir Thomas Picton School

WAR!

People
unsuspecting.
Suddenly Hitler is
dropping bombs, messengers
of death.

Hannah Rastall (12)
Sir Thomas Picton School

PEACE

Silence,
No screams or cries,
No more bombs exploding,
Now everything is completely
Peaceful.

Sarah Nicholls (12)
Sir Thomas Picton School

WAR

Sirens
makin' noises
like noisy buzzing
bees
all fighting in a
fearful swarm
in war.

Hannah Evans (12)
Sir Thomas Picton School

WAR

Oh no!
They've come again,
What will happen
this time?
How many houses
will be bombed?
Darkness!

Kelly-Anne Davies (13)
Sir Thomas Picton School

AIR RAIDS

Air Raids
Mean planes bombing
Houses being destroyed
Later on, noises turn into
Silence!

Luke Hughes (12)
Sir Thomas Picton School

WAR!

Bombs drop
Houses shattered
Everyone is screaming
And on the distant horizon
Silence!

Rachel Horne (12)
Sir Thomas Picton School

WAR

Bombers
Fly overhead
As they drop their bombs
Ruining the houses
they see.
Germans!

Simon Lewis (12)
Sir Thomas Picton School

WAR

I cry,
I've got to leave,
It is too dangerous,
I don't want to leave
my mother.
I'm sad.

Gemma Jones (12)
Sir Thomas Picton School

WAR

Sirens
Wail all night long
Wake people from their sleep
They come running to the shelter
Waiting.

Eleanor Richards (12)
Sir Thomas Picton School

WAR

Air raids
Dingy shelters
Small children are frightened
Adults in a dreadful hurry
Then calm!

Gemma Bevan (12)
Sir Thomas Picton School

WAR!

War starts
Bombs start to drop
People get in shelters
Everybody is terrified
All gone.

Sarah McPherson (12)
Sir Thomas Picton School

PEACE

Laughing
Everything safe
Nothing to be scared of
Everything about is quiet
Peaceful.

Kim Dunlop (12)
Sir Thomas Picton School

PEACE

We've won
Germans have gone
Peaceful nights, sleeping tight
Waves breaking on the shore, sun shines
Peace again.

Samantha Bevan (12)
Sir Thomas Picton School

PEACE

It's Peace.
No guns, no war
No bombs, no planes, no pain
Just silence! No hatred,
No death.
It's Peace!

Tom Chaloner (12)
Sir Thomas Picton School

WAR

Dark room
Lonely people
The air raid sirens are
Loud and clear. Guns banging
loud, then
Silence!

Amy Archer (12)
Sir Thomas Picton School

WAR

Bomb hits
Street is shattered
What is happening
now?
How many people
will be killed?
Silence!

Anne-Marie Bentley (12)
Sir Thomas Picton School

PEACE

Love is
contentment and
happiness with others,
have hope today, peace for the
future.

Hayley Reeves (13)
Sir Thomas Picton School

WAR POEM

The shocked faces stare over the
sea of motionless bodies.
Ruined buildings, crumpled
like paper no longer wanted.
Streets filled with bleakness and
the hatred hard not to notice.
Tears rolling over mothers' cheeks
like leaves falling from an
autumn tree.
The streets are still and the
bodies unwanted as families return
to their cold empty houses.

Alice Lewis (13)
Sir Thomas Picton School

FUTURE VOICES

In the beginning this world was pretty,
No pollution, no cars, no man,
There was nothing to hurt the ozone
And no litter, not even a tin can.

But now it is changed
In every which way,
There's pollution, there's cars, there's man
And the world is a toy with which man can play.

It should not be like this,
It should be peaceful once again,
Just birds and trees all over the place,
Not only women and men.

Christopher Clare (12)
Ysgol Uwchradd Tregaron

MY VOICE

In a shrunken world I wait for it to pass,
As I stand in a room made out of glass.
I think about the future and how it will be,
But still I think it could be ugly.

In this shrunken world I wait in agony,
Waiting for someone to release me.
I think of my life and how it used to be,
Until I got stuck in here and turned ugly.

This world is strange and covered in grass,
All of my friends have turned to glass.
I see their faces glistening in the sun,
Wondering 'What have we done?'

I'm freed from that room of glass,
I look around to find no grass.
All I see is a destroyed world I hoped had passed,

Oh how I wish I was back in that room of glass.

Christina Gray (13)
Ysgol Uwchradd Tregaron

FUTURE VOICES

The millennium is on its way again
And what's the great big deal
It's driving most people insane
And that's all it is, another day!

They want foxes killed no more
And what about the fifty pence sheep?
The Fresian bull calves are not worth even a sweet
And politics are up the creek!

Poor Kosovo, what a mess
Their own country turned against them.
Turkey are shaking in some patches
And the states are having twisters in batches!

Wales are hoping to hold the wonderful World Cup
Going into a mysterious millennium.
I just hope it will build a better life
For me, for you, and for everyone.

Jennifer Claire Davies (12)
Ysgol Uwchradd Tregaron

MILLENNIUM AND WALES

Millennium is coming
It's come so fast,
enjoy it while it lasts
and forget the past
because it will go fast.

What will the millennium
mean to Wales?
Millennium Bugs
millennium babies
haps and daffodils
Welsh ladies.

Will the rugby team be better?
Will the world get any smaller?
Robots, earthquakes, wars and bugs
millennium capsules, coins and mugs.

Carys Davies (8)
Ysgol Uwchradd Tregaron

HOW WILL IT BE?

Will we have earthquakes in the next millennium?
Will aliens be in charge of Ten Downing Street?

Will we have pocket money or a plastic card?
Will I pay in pounds or will it be Euros?

Will archaeologists discover something new?
Will we be living in space?

Will we have a third world war?
Will we have robots attending us?

Will we have sunshine?
Will we have rain?

Will we be eating beef and lamb?
Will we be vegetarians?

Will we be using cars or trains?
Will we be cycling or catching planes?

Will we wear spacesuits?
Will we wear wool?

In the next millennium how will it be?
We'll have to sit tight, wait and see!

Emyr Davies (12)
Ysgol Uwchradd Tregaron

FUTURE VOICES

In the future will it all change?
Will there be pollution,
A new evolution?
Will man discover new worlds
And start a space age?

Will there be world peace?
People will look to the past,
Digging up old memories to last.
In years to come man will live in space.
Is this the future for the human race?

Joseph Williams
Ysgol Uwchradd Tregaron

FUTURE VOICES

I look out of my window
and I see the trees blowing,
children are playing
(and that's what I see out of the window).

I look to the left,
I look to the right
and what do I see?
Is the future bright?

Poetry, writing,
athletics and swimming
and all I like doing is
playing and playing.

Some day it can be really quiet,
another it can be a real riot.
The voices can be scary,
(but I get really frightened) and incidents so hairy!

I hope you like my poem
and you should do one too.
Poetry is a great thing
so try it, it's a great thing to do.

Claire Davies
Ysgol Uwchradd Tregaron

FUTURE VOICES

At night, when all is dark,
I look at the stars
And wonder will they stay there,
Until the world comes to an end.

Will there be more?
Will there be less?
Will they disappear,
Or will they stay there?

Will the moon disappear?
Will the sun die?
Will they live,
Or will they stay for another day?

We don't know what will happen next,
So let's just hold on and wait and see.

Emma Stevens (12)
Ysgol Uwchradd Tregaron

FUTURE VOICES

I would like it if children's voices could be heard
All over the entire world.
Even adults would have to listen,
Listen carefully to every word.

Adults would have to do some chores
And go to school every day,
So we could stay at home
And go outside and play.

Caryl Davies (12)
Ysgol Uwchradd Tregaron

WHAT WILL THE WORLD BE LIKE?

When I was younger, six or seven,
I didn't know what it would be like when I was eleven.
It was very different in ninety-three,
You wouldn't see a PlayStation or wide screen TV.

I'm twelve now and I'm thinking again
Of what it will be like in two thousand and ten.
Will we have alien pen pals far up in the stars?
Will astronauts set foot on Venus or Mars?

Will the world be different or will it be the same?
Will virtual reality be the only way to play a game?
Will there be world peace or will there still be wars?
Will there still be crime and will there still be laws?

We'll possibly find out the answers sometime,
I hope you liked my little rhyme.

Joe Roberts (12)
Ysgol Uwchradd Tregaron

FUTURE VOICES

The new millennium is nearly here
Celebrating with parties and music
Thinking of the homeless and the poor
Wishing for peace around the world
Talking about the Millennium Bug!
It could cause lots of havoc
Computers going down all over the world
The world could come to an end
With aliens and robots there to attend.

Catrin Jones (12)
Ysgol Uwchradd Tregaron

FUTURE VOICES

In the future we all hope for
no hunger, no pollution and definitely no war,
a place of peace, a place of warmth,
a place where racism is no more.

In the future we all hope for
a cure for AIDS, being a curse no more,
a cure for cancer,
which strikes daily behind many a door.

In the future we all hope for
many more planets to go and explore,
a walk on Venus, a walk on Mars,
to see close up, the beautiful stars.

Peter Horton (13)
Ysgol Uwchradd Tregaron

FUTURE VOICES

F   uture is tomorrow,
U   nknown galaxies,
T   o discover undiscovered places,
U   nknown distances away,
R   einhabitate these places,
E   ven as tomorrow will come.

V   oices calling
O   ut our names,
I   n the distant winds,
C   onscious minds conjuring,
E   choing the memories,
S   creaming out towards us.

Gwenan Arch (8)
Ysgol Uwchradd Tregaron

FUTURE VOICES

Peace not war
The millennium, a new door
Politics, passions, people and fashions
Children pray for famine to go away
We sit and play computers all day
Bits and megabytes rot our brain
Global warming, acid rain
Sci-fi is taking over our telly
Junk food, bloating every belly
Voices shout 'It's time for change'
2000 echoes, the new and strange
Satellites, inventions, discovery and more
This is the future
Peace not war.

Mark Leese (13)
Ysgol Uwchradd Tregaron

TOMORROW

Tomorrow's world is a day away,
why live for then, why not today?
The future is a scary place,
we must give way to the future race.
We have no choice, we all must die,
no one has the right to be forever alive.
Stay happy while you're on this earth,
right up to your death, right from your birth.
Smile today at the passers-by
and try your best to keep your head high.
Be proud of who you are inside
because we are all beautiful in our own right.

Grace Acres (14)
Ysgol Uwchradd Tregaron

FUTURE VOICES

Out of my window I can see,
Plants, gardens and a tree.

The road is full of noisy cars
And means to travel to the stars.

Well kept gardens but my fear,
How will it look when I'm not here?

Children coming home from school,
Will computers come and rule?

Cardiff's own Millennium Stadium,
People visit by the million.

Classroom full of noisy children,
Robots ruling by the trillion!

Daniel Williams (12)
Ysgol Uwchradd Tregaron

ENVIRONMENT IN THE NEW MILLENNIUM

E ndangered animals
N ature destroyed
V ehicles polluting
I llness from drugs and alcohol
R adio activity
O zone hole
N oise pollutions
M anmade disasters
E nergy waste
N atural disasters
T he Millennium Bug.

Robert Hockey (15)
Ysgol Uwchradd Tregaron

THE FUTURE VOICES

Will I be part of the future?
Will I have something to offer?
I might be the new Tony Blair
Or maybe a huge movie star!

The beaches will turn into rubbish tips
Graffiti all over the walls
The world taken over by robots
Or maybe the sun will explode.

Will classical music be more popular?
Maybe Bryn Terfel will be on 'Top of the Pops'
Shirley Bassey at Number One and,
The Spice Girls struggling to reach the top 40!

Will World War III ever start?
Will there be more nuclear bombs?
Maybe an asteroid will hit the Earth
Will the world be a better place?

I wonder what the fashion will be like
Will red and pink be the matching colours?
Maybe tight-fit jeans will be the new hipsters
And no one wearing platforms.

Will everything come to a halt
As the clock strikes on the eve of the millennium?
I hope I will be here to see
What the future holds for me.

Rebecca Pugh (13)
Ysgol Uwchradd Tregaron

FUTURE VOICES

The world could be a better place,
Think of it,
It could be ace.
Let's make a resolution,
To start with no pollution.
No wars, just peace,
No school uniform,
But a good education.
That would be a sensation.
A children's vote for over twelve years
And places for the homeless.
Children should get parent benefits
And don't forget a proper cure for nits!
Racism is a 'big' no, no,
Guns and hunting have got to go!
To stop the world from looking bitter,
There should be a '£10' fine for dropping litter!
People should treat each other respectfully,
Animals should be treated with love and care,
The way life is now just isn't fair.
So together to stop the tears
And many people's fears.
We'll make the world brilliant
In a couple of years.

Laura Regan (12)
Ysgol Uwchradd Tregaron